PRINCES RISBOROUGH PAST

High Street, *c.*1915. This tranquil view, published by W.E. Fisher from his chemist's shop in the Market Square, shows the *George & Dragon* on the left and the early 20th-century post office on the right. Beyond that is the archway leading to Ayres' Farm and further still, the high roof of the Literary Institute. In the distance, above the former *White Lion*, are the Chiltern foothills, which were then the fields of Town Farm but are now filled with houses.

PRINCES RISBOROUGH PAST

Sandy Macfarlane & Chris Kingham

Phillimore

1997

Published by
PHILLIMORE & CO. LTD.
Shopwyke Manor Barn, Chichester, West Sussex

ISBN 1 86077 047 9

Printed and bound in Great Britain by
BUTLER & TANNER LTD.
London and Frome

Contents

List of Illustrations

Frontispiece: High Street, *c.*1915

Acknowledgements

The following have kindly allowed the reproduction of drawings and photographs: Michael Adamson, 90, 91, 92, 93; William Barnard, 35, 133; The Bodleian Library, 5, 53; The British Legion, 143; Buckinghamshire County Library and Record Office, 24, 77; *Bucks Herald*, 156, 159; Country Life Picture Library, 25, 26; A.B. Demaus, 123, 124; Mrs. M. Digweed, 36, 100, 106; David East, 72, 95, 132; John East, 112; Ronald Goodearl, 57, 62, 97, 113; Hunting Aerofilms, 158; Dr. and Mrs. P. Kennedy, 105; Tom Kingham, 142; Mr. & Mrs. A. Laidler, 104; Mrs. P. Lidgley, 128; The National Portrait Gallery, London, 20; The Pettigrove family, 49; The Editor, *Records of Buckinghamshire*, 21, 22, 23; Michael Smith, 81, 103; Mrs. K. Stow, 117; Mrs. S. Telfer, 131; The Victoria and Albert Museum, 34; J. Wainwright, 158; Mervyn Wallen, 89; Arthur Witcher, 94, 155; Mrs. D.B. Witney, 149; and, last but by no means least, the Wood family of Town Farm, 29, 73, 111, 134, 135, 138, 139, 151, 152.

All other illustrations come from the authors' collections or the society's archive. If any copyright permission has been inadvertently overlooked we apologise and ask for forgiveness.

The authors particularly wish to thank their wives, without whose support and forbearance this book would not have come to fruition.

1 'Nestling in the vale it stands beneath the hills, whereon the cross uplifted high looks down.' The Oxford photographer Henry Taunt's view from the manor park in 1868. Nowadays all the hillside in the background is covered in trees and scrub.

Foreword

On 13 September 1906 this delightful 'Week-end impression, No. XVII' appeared in the *Evening Standard* and *St James's Gazette*:

> When there are two ways from the station, one by road, the other by a field path, does not a ruralising Londoner delight—if he is quite sure he is not trespassing—to take the latter? It is doubly fortunate that there are two ways from the station of Princes Risborough to the village, for by taking the path one avoids those new-looking, entirely unpicturesque cottages on which the eye lights at first glance, not precisely with pleasure. Somewhat anxious to see how the village looks on closer inspection, one crosses the meadows, and reaches a little gate, where the fruitful boughs of apple trees hang above the path. A dozen paces more, and one arrives unexpectedly in the market place, where a survey of the village can be conveniently made. With relief one notices many a pleasing touch of character—a church on whose weather-stained spire is a vane that leans out of the perpendicular, here a grape-vine flourishing on decrepit walls, there a bit of herring-bone brickwork, pavements of cobbles, and a market-house on pillars, neither a large nor handsome building, but suggestive of a bygone life. This is Princes Risborough, an ancient village … today brought into a workaday world by a brand-new main line of railway.

It is still a delight to walk this route into the town, as we now call it, though the field path has become an avenue of houses and the church boasts a new spire. Rosewood Cottage in The Butts is unchanged, though the apple tree is hard-pruned, and as one wends one's way to the market square the atmosphere is still redolent of bygone days.

This book also attempts to follow an enjoyable path. Any pretensions it may have had to being the definitive history of Princes Risborough were quickly dispelled for it was soon apparent that a wealth of information remains to be uncovered. Rather, by taking a broad view it hopes to show how Risborough present is the child of Risborough past.

No attempt has been made to analyse every aspect of life in the town, nor are there chapters devoted to the past or present hamlets, which are all deserving of their own studies. Several such works already published are referred to in the text and the authors would not wish, in the evocative words of the Rev. John Shepherd in 1819, 'to cramp the hand of the industrious cottager' who might be contemplating an account of his or her immediate locality or interest.

2 Rosewood Cottage and Winterfold guard the gateway to the town from the manor park. This photo was taken *c.*1908, soon after the modern spire was built.

3 The cobbled pavement of Church Street. The gabled frontage in the right foreground, now a separate shop, was part of the early 19th-century 'vicarage' and later a doctor's surgery. The vine in the background was planted in 1879.

4 Children gather in Church Street, flanked on the left by jettied cottages with 15th-century elements and on the right by Cromwell House, dating from the early 17th century. In the background is the chimney of the Lion brewery, demolished in 1927.

Although every effort has been made to verify what is presented by examination of original material, the task of unravelling the past has been made easier by reference to the published and unpublished work of other historians and by the guidance of the Buckinghamshire county archivists and librarians.[1]

Equally valuable has been the willing help of the many people of Princes Risborough who have allowed access to their documents, homes and memories. In acknowledging this debt the society hopes to have repaid it in some measure by providing a sufficiently interesting and reliable foundation for further study.

Princes Risborough Past is the first publication of the Princes Risborough Area Heritage Society and any ensuing income will be devoted to promoting the aims of the society. The background research has been jointly undertaken by Chris Kingham, the society's Archivist, and Sandy Macfarlane, its President. The latter is particularly grateful to Mr. Eric Danbury and the late Mr. Brian Dowley for commenting and advising on his text but accepts responsibility for any inaccuracies.

[1] For the sake of convenience the following abbreviations are used in the footnotes:
BRO   Buckinghamshire Records Office
Rec. Bucks.   Records of Buckinghamshire
Hist. Buck.   *History and Antiquities of the County of Buckingham*

Chapter One

Out of the Mist

PRINCES RISBOROUGH stands at approximately 100m. (328ft.) above sea-level in the broad northern mouth of one of the few gaps in the 60-mile length of the Chiltern Hills allowing easy passage between the flat-lands to the north and the London basin to the south. On either side of this gap the land rises steeply to the escarpment, marked by Bledlow Cop to the west and Kop Hill, at a height of 250m. (820ft.), to the east.

This geographical formation at times gives rise to a wonderful natural phenomenon, when in the early morning one can look down from the summit of Kop Hill onto a carpet of mist which fills the gap, pierced only by a few landmarks such as the spire of St Mary's Church, as Baron Munchhausen's pierced the snow. Looking down on the scene one can only guess at what else lies beneath the mist. So it is with the earliest history of the town, a few silent relics giving tantalising glimpses of the distant past.

One such relic is the pudding-stone which today stands by the roundabout at the foot of New Road Hill. By the time the Ice Ages had drawn to a close in about 8000 BC the melt-water from glaciers retreating from the Chiltern escarpment had shaped and deposited many such sedimentary conglomerate boulders in the region. Added to their geological

5   Looking west from Whiteleaf Cross, c.1910.

6   The Risborough gap from Bledlow Cop to Whiteleaf Cross, in 1742. On the extreme right is Lodge Hill, and the Lower Icknield Way winds across the fields on the left. The windmill just right of centre was taken down in the late 18th century. The little wooded hill to the left of it marks Parkfield. (Bodleian Library Rawl. 4o. 52. opp. p.34)

7   Almost the same view in the 1980s, with the houses of Bledlow Road, Saunderton, in the right mid-ground and the Upper Icknield Way behind them.

significance is the belief that they were used as way-markers by early man. How long did this one stand in increasing obscurity in Back Lane before being restored to prominence when the road was improved in 1984?

Although it is clear from the flint implements they left behind that people were moving through the Chilterns throughout the immense span of the Early Stone Age, the earliest visible features are barrows to be found on both sides of the Risborough Gap, some of which date from the late Neolithic and early Bronze Ages, roughly 2600-1200 BC. The most readily apparent and best-documented of these is the ovoid Neolithic long barrow above Whiteleaf Cross[1] which was excavated in 1934-9, revealing post-holes suggestive of a burial chamber, and thought to be older than the two round barrows whose remnants lie to the north-west of it. It is being badly eroded although it has been suggested

9　The puddingstone boulder, recovered from the former Back Lane and a symbol of pre-history.

10　The Neolithic barrow above Whiteleaf Cross. The damage done by feet and tyres, aggravated by rain, is only too apparent.

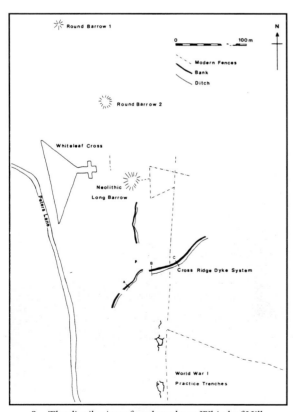

8　The distribution of earthworks on Whiteleaf Hill.

that in its present form it represents back-filling after the excavation rather than the original barrow.

It seems appropriate to discuss Whiteleaf Cross itself at this point, if only to say that it appears to be of no great antiquity. The earliest known representation of it was done for the antiquarian, Browne Willis, in 1742 and entitled *Crux Saxonica*[2] but at the time 'Saxon' was a description freely applied to many features of unknown origin. It seems impossible to believe that so prominent a feature would have escaped comment at an earlier date if it had been in existence. If one ignores the triangular base, which may be a natural geological feature, it is almost identical with the cross at Bledlow, which similarly lacks early records.

In 1983 a crouched burial was found in a garden in Clifford Road. It was also thought to be late

11   Whiteleaf Cross from Peters Lane, *c.*1915.

12   Bledlow Cross from the Henton junction.

13 Hidden in the trees, at the left of the summit of Pulpit Hill, is an Iron-Age hill fort. Below it is Grangelands, a Berks, Bucks and Oxon Naturalists' Trust (BBONT) chalk downland reserve where butterflies and flowers thrive.

Neolithic or slightly later, within the range *c.*2100-1500 BC in radio-carbon years.[3] No barrow was identified, not surprisingly in what is a landscaped and previously agricultural area, but interestingly enough a former track connecting the town to Culverton at this level on the hillside was called the Barrow Way.

The late Bronze to early Iron Ages are represented by the hill-fort on the top of Pulpit Hill to the north-east of Risborough. The site has not been studied in detail but it is thought to have been used as a temporary refuge in times of trouble. Its ditches and ramparts enclose some 3½ acres. Although much reduced by filling and erosion and extensively covered by beech trees and scrub these are still impressive. Where the site remains open, the view over the Vale of Aylesbury is breathtaking.

The late Iron Age saw the arrival of the Romans and Julius Caesar's two expeditions in 55-4 BC. There is ample evidence of Roman settlement and, indeed, of Romano-British integration in the area, with Belgic sites and Roman villas known to have existed at Bledlow, Lodge Hill and Saunderton.

The Saunderton site was excavated by the Buckinghamshire Archaeological Society directed

14 Pulpit Hill fort.

15 Pulpit Hill fort, showing how nature is trying to reclaim the land.

16   Looking north over the Vale of Aylesbury from Pulpit Hill. Great Kimble church is at centre foreground and Waddesdon Manor, 10 miles distant, is on the skyline, to the left.

by Diana Ashcroft in 1938.[4] Lack of funds limited the period of study to three-and-a-half weeks after which the site was covered over to await further exploration, but it revealed a villa thought to have been a dwelling built in c.AD 150, replacing a first-century one. However, after further discoveries of walls, a coloured floor and other artefacts by Mr. Messer of Church Farm and Mr. Frank Pavry of Bledlow, the site was re-assessed in 1969 by Keith Branigan,[5] later appointed Professor of Prehistory and Archaeology at Sheffield University. He felt that marble slabs and chalk tesserae from the earlier villa indicated too fine a building to have been replaced solely by that excavated in 1938 and that the latter was an outbuilding belonging to a much larger and as yet undiscovered villa of which the new finds were a fragment.

The excavated villa fell into decay during the third century but was repaired early in the fourth. For a time in the mid-fourth century it was abandoned but was again occupied for an unknown

but probably brief period into the early fifth century. By then Rome had formally severed its connections with the island and the Celtic British population was left to confront a succession of 'barbarian' invaders, notably the Anglo-Saxons, and over the next four hundred years or so merge with them. Of these Dark Ages, so important to the shaping of the region, little is known. Saxon burials, such as those at Bledlow where the suffix *-low* is derived from the Saxon word for barrow, are almost the only source of information in the Risborough area, but the advent of Christianity (with the see at Dorchester founded in AD 635) diminished their value through the absence of grave goods. However, the County Archaeological Department has in recent years shed considerable light on the settlement at Walton in Aylesbury.

It is in this era that the names of both the region and the town first appear, the first as a relic of the past and the second given by the invaders. In his pioneering work on the Chiltern region during this

17 The Saunderton Roman villa during excavation in 1938, looking east.

period Rutherford Davis[6] discusses the identity of the *Cilternsaetan*, the Chiltern folk mentioned in the seventh-century Tribal Hidage, and the derivation of the name from a Celtic British adjective *-celto*, meaning 'high'. He also points out that while compound settlement names with suffixes such as *-wic* (farm) and *-ham* (village) appear early, the majority of names in the Chiltern zone are topographically descriptive. So it is with Risborough, the brush-covered hills or 'hrisebeorgan' of the Anglo-Saxon. It is interesting to note the spelling 'hrise' and a progression from Domesday Book 'rise' to 'rys' and then, by Elizabethan times, 'ris' and to wonder if it was once pronounced with a long 'i'.

During the ninth and 10th centuries, perhaps because of Viking or, more specifically, Danish incursion, the administrative divisions known as 'hundreds', based on estates, began to give way to towns. The memory of those once important units lives on in the device whereby Members of Parliament retire by appointment to the stewardship of the Chiltern Hundreds which include Desborough to which Risborough belonged before later becoming one of the three Hundreds of Aylesbury.

By the end of the 10th century, estate or parish boundaries were well defined with the typical Chiltern shape being a long strip running lengthwise from the vale up into the hills. Princes Risborough was no exception though the earliest complete account of its bounds is an 18th-century copy of a survey said to have been taken in AD 1620.[7] Part at least of its ancient boundaries can be assumed from those of Monks Risborough in a copy of an earlier account dated AD 903, analysed in detail by Arnold Baines.[8] The stage was now set for the Norman Conquest and the second millennium.

Chapter Two

King's Manor and Abbot's Hold

WHEN DUKE WILLIAM of Normandy conquered England in 1066 his army passed close by Risborough on its way from Wallingford to Berkhamsted. William took over an efficient administration which he later put to good use in the compilation of what was soon known as Domesday Book, a comprehensive survey of his domain begun in 1085 and completed within a year. In it,[1] (Princes) Risborough is described as land of the king, formerly a village of Earl Harold, 30 hides in all. Reckoning a hide at 120 acres gives a figure of 3,600 acres which approximates to the 3,900 acres with a further 500 acres of common or waste land measured in 1810 prior to enclosure of the parish.

There were said to be 30 villagers, 12 smallholders, three slaves and a Freeman holding three virgates (90 acres, but in strips). It has been

18 Park Mill, Summerleys Road, descended from one of the two mills mentioned in Domesday Book. No longer a working mill, the mill race has been incorporated into the present-day house.

19 The Lacey Green windmill in 1920, soon after it had ceased to turn after almost 100 years on this site. Subsequently it almost disintegrated but has now been restored to its former glory under the auspices of the Chiltern Society.

suggested[2] that to allow for wives and children these figures should be multiplied four or five times, giving an estimated population for Risborough of about two hundred. There were two mills and sufficient woodland for 1,000 pigs. A burgess of Oxford paid dues and a salt-boiler of Droitwich rendered an unspecified number of loads of salt which led Leonard Bull to suggest, in discussing a possible salt road from Droitwich to Hedsor Wharf on the Thames,[3] that Risborough might already have been a trading centre at that date.

The Domesday mills are thought to have been represented by Culverton Mill, destroyed by fire in the 1960s, and Park Mill, no longer a working mill but converted into a house. Longwick Mill was added somewhat later. All three were watermills, taking their power from the stream arising near Culverton Farm at Pyrtle spring. Formerly called Purtwell, its flow is so reduced today, aggravated by break-up of the bed of the stream, that it is difficult to imagine how important it was to the community.

A windmill once overlooked Pyrtle spring from the shoulder of the hill to the north east and can be seen in the 1742 drawing (plate 5). It had gone by the end of the 18th century, soon to be replaced by the famous smock mill at Lacey Green, brought from Chesham in 1821. Although moving a mill might seem an unlikely undertaking, even earlier, c.1650, a windmill from Risborough was taken to Radnage. This was probably the Monks Risborough windmill, thought to have stood in the field north of Kingsmead where a mound of sorts is just visible.

Monks Risborough also had a watermill and the house remains in Mill Lane. There used also to be a smaller one, Cut Mill, on the other side of the present railway, between Mill Lane and Alscot. All the above were predominantly corn mills while North Mill at Bledlow and, for much of its life, Saunderton Mill were paper mills.

Risborough, then, had been a royal manor before the Conquest and half of it remained so until 1628 when Charles I conveyed it to the City of London in part payment of debts. For the sake of

10

clarity this half will be called the King's Manor. The other half descended to Walter Giffard, Earl of Buckinghamshire, who, in about 1162, granted the church tithes and advowson (the right of appointment to the living), together with an unidentified wood called Lullesled, to the Abbey of Notley. The abbey also seems to have held most of Speen, a house called Brooke House with Cannon Close nearby, the whole being known as the Manor of Brooke, Abbot's Manor or Hold.

The separation has led to considerable historical confusion, the more so after 1539 when the Abbey of Notley was dissolved by Henry VIII who reclaimed the Abbot's Manor and eventually granted it to the Bishop of Oxford. Elizabeth I recovered it and, while continuing to allow the church its tithes and other dues, later granted the manor to the Hampdens.[4] They were related by marriage to the Giffards and in that sense the wheel had turned full circle.

It is known that from at least 1305 the King's Manor consisted in the main of a stud farm and deer park, for in that year an order to the bailiffs of Queen Margaret, wife of Edward I, confirmed the right of the Abbot of Notley to tithes of colts and money from agistment (a charge for grazing) in the park. In 1325 Edward II ordered a house to be built for the stud which by then had taken over the park completely.

Edward III appointed his eldest son Edward, the Black Prince, custodian of the manor in 1343. A letter in the Register of the Black Prince indicates that he visited his manor at least once, in 1359: 'be pleased to know that Sir John de Hide came to us at our manor at Risebergh … given under our signet at the said manor'.[5] The town, already important enough to be called Great (magna), became known as *Princes* Rysburgh (principis), a distinction not accorded to others of the Prince's manors in the county and mainly to distinguish it from its neighbour Monks Risborough (monachorum).

Tradition held that the Prince had a 'palace' at a site west of St Mary's Church called The Mount, today a car park. In 1955 excavations carried out on this site uncovered the remains of two adjacent

20 Edward, the Black Prince, 1330-76. (By courtesy of the National Portrait Gallery, London)

blocks of buildings, not necessarily of contemporary origin but together forming a substantial manor house with walls of flint or witchert, a mixture of chalk mud and straw still to be found today, notably at Haddenham.

The findings at the Mount were comprehensively reported.[6] They showed that the site had been in use from at least the 13th century but that the main period of occupation of the buildings themselves was during the 14th century. By the early 15th century they had either been drastically altered

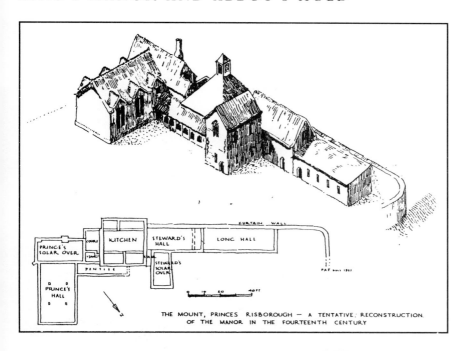

21 A suggested reconstruction of the Black Prince's manor at The Mount.

22 *(right)*   The Askett manor before demolition.

23 *(below)*   A reconstruction of the Askett manor timber frame.

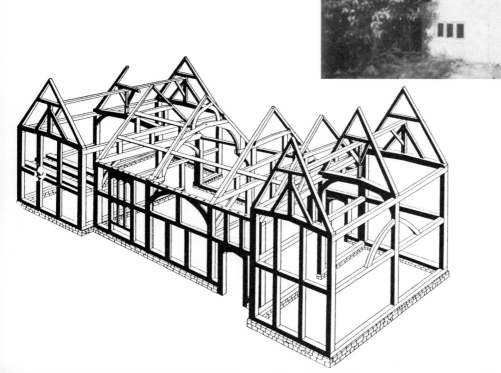

or destroyed. A comparable Manor House used to stand on the left of the eastern end of Crowbrook Road at Askett.[7] It was of similar age but greater sophistication, and survived until 1969 when, having been much altered over the years, it was demolished as derelict and unsafe.

The investigators appear to have hoped to find some trace of the Brooke House of the Abbot's Manor at the Mount, encouraged by Lipscomb who said that 'the site and contiguous lands, having been granted to the Hampdens in the reign of Elizabeth, descended ... [to] George Robert Hobart-Hampden,

24   Brooke House in 1824.

25   The Manor House in 1935 after restoration by the Rothschilds. (The Country Life Picture Library)

Earl of Buckinghamshire, who caused the decayed mansion to be taken down'. However, the Earl did not succeed to the title until 1816 and a hundred years earlier Nathaniel Anderson, minister of St Mary's, had told the antiquarian Browne Willis that the Black Prince 'had a palace near the church; which is now totally demollifhed: and nothing but Corn and grass grows wh[ere] this famous palace once stood'.[8] Also, the only traces of occupation at the Mount as late as the 17th and 18th centuries were a few stone-ware sherds near the entrance to the site.

In the same letter of *c*.1715 Nathaniel Anderson said that about threescore years earlier 'this parsonage' [i.e. the living] had been in the possession of one Mrs. Chibnall, a Widow Gentlewoman, and that the house she had lived in with her daughter Mary, and now in possession of the Lord of the manor, Henry Penton, had been called Brooke

House but was now most commonly called the Parsonage House.

The present Manor House is said to date from 1630-50 as an early example of a later 17th-century type.[9] If so it was almost certainly built for Mrs. Chibnall and the house in which Anderson says she was living *c*.1655. He does not mention another which might fit the bill, only saying that there were houses adjacent to the church, for the poor. It seems reasonable to conclude that the original Brooke House was then already decayed and it may be that the present building replaced it. The interior wall running parallel to the front wall is said to be of earlier construction than the rest and may be a remnant of the older house.[10] It is also said that the stairway and balustrade which are the crowning glory of the present building are older than the rest and even that the house was designed for the stairway

26 A detail of the magnificent Jacobean balustrade, each panel carved from solid wood. (The Country Life Picture Library)

rather than vice-versa. It seems more likely that a local craftsman simply continued working in an old style, not unusual in rural areas. An exquisite 17th-century longcase clock at Chequers, by John Hill of Risborough, shows the quality of craftsmanship available locally.

Joan Chibnall was a wealthy and generous woman from a well-landed family called Adeane. She is remembered for Chibnall's Charity, now consolidated with other town charities but established by her will of 1646 to provide gowns for 'poor widows or ancient ladies' of Princes Risborough and Chalgrove, Britwell and Watlington where the family also had estates. She had acquired an interest in the Abbot's manor as security for a loan made by her to the previous lord, John Jackman, and she and her steward bought it outright in 1624. Then, in 1631, she also bought the King's manor from

the City of London. After this the two manors had one lord though separate courts continued for some time, dealing mainly with matters of tenancy.[11]

It is interesting that many of the changes of ownership arose from debt or bankruptcy. Mrs. Chibnall was succeeded by her nephew, Thomas Adeane. At his death he left a balance of debts and legal costs of some £4,600 and when this was settled in Chancery the manor was bought, in about 1700, by Henry Penton. (Lipscomb says Elizabeth I called on Mr. Penton at Brooke House when visiting Hampden, surely an anachronism.) It has also been said that the portrait painter, Sir Peter Lely, bought the manor in 1671 but it seems that his connection was simply to be paid a rent from the manor fee-farm by conveyance from citizens of London.

John Grubb bought what was effectively the Abbot's manor in 1762 but the Penton family kept

the King's manor until the early 19th century. It was then also sold, by a later Henry Penton who was born in Winchester and was its sometime Member of Parliament. It is for this reason that many important documents relating to both manors are to be found in Hampshire Record Office in Winchester, though they are gradually being made available on microfilm in the Buckinghamshire Record Office.[12]

In 1841 the above-mentioned John Grubb's great-nephew, another John, sold the manors to the Duke of Buckingham and, after a few more changes of ownership, they were conveyed to James Cuddon in 1858. He is the last confirmed lord of the manors though his agent, Humphrey Bull, did make a claim. It seems likely that by then, with changes in the nature of tenancy and major sales of land, lordship of the manors had become a title without substance.

What was the town like in the 17th-18th centuries? According to a marginal note in Anderson's letter there were more than one hundred families but it is not clear if this means in the whole parish, for he adds that Longwick has 'well nigh 40'. Building was regulated, as shown by a presentation to the Manor Court on 4 May 1693 that 'there is a new Erected Cottage wherein Francis JENKINS now dwelleth sett up neere the Windmill [near Pyrtle Spring] by one (...) VERE whereto there is not four acres of freehold Land laid to itt'.

Within the town and parish were said to be 88 copyhold tenements. Of these, 26 were farmhouses, with barns and outhouses, and Town Farm in Church Street presumably represents one of them. Two other farms disappeared from within the town in the early 1900s: Ayres' farm, converted into business premises on the north side of the High

27 *(above left)*　The Old Vicarage or Monks Staithe.

28 *(below left)*　Cromwell House in Church Street, as it is today, carefully restored from a state of extreme distress under a scheme established in 1969 by the then County Architect, F. Pooley. The twin gables, mullion and transom first-floor windows and Flemish bond brickwork are characteristic of the 17th century.

29 *(right)*　Town Farm, *c.*1909, with Mrs. Wood, her three sons, Stan, Ron and Reg and their cousin Connie. Note the Flemish bond brickwork and the fire insurance sign which was rudely stolen some years ago.

30   Mrs. Ayres and her nephew, Herbert Rogers, outside Ayres' Farm in the High Street, c.1885.

31   Part of the catalogue when Ayres' Farm was sold by Herbert Rogers in 1904. The archway into the former farmyard, with its projecting stones to protect the walls from cart wheels, still exists and can be seen in the frontispiece.

Street, and Williams' farm, which burnt down, on the south. There were 62 dwelling houses, with seven more 'which about three yeares since [1698] were burnt downe, but are now Rebuilt'.[13] One can only guess at the whereabouts and identity of those 'Antient Coppyhold Tenements'.

Only a few buildings dating from or before the 17th century still survive. They include St Mary's Church and the Manor House, though both have been significantly altered in the last two hundred years. Opposite, and older than, the Manor House is the cottage once known as the Old Vicarage and more recently as Monk's Staithe, best-known for having once been the home of the pioneer aviatrix, Amy Johnson.

Several cottages adjoining the churchyard, Nathaniel Anderson's 'church houses', were demolished in the 18th century when the workhouse was built and more went in the 19th century when the workhouse itself was pulled down. Fortunately, of a row of cottages in Church Street condemned as unfit for habitation in the 1930s, all but two survive. Converted into the Parrott Hall, named after the local solicitor who organised their rescue, the cottages were for a time the headquarters of the fire brigade. Later, between 1956-86, they housed the local branch of the county library and when that was superseded by the present library they became a restaurant.

Cromwell House, in Church Street, was rescued from a state of neglect by the County Council in 1972. Its twin-gabled façade is of a style popular in the early 1600s and its external appearance has probably changed little, with original brickwork and first-floor windows and faithfully reproduced modern timbers framing original glass in the gables.

The Gables, in the Market Square, dates from the same era but its original herring-bone brickwork and timber framing have been replaced by a modern façade. It is tempting to identify the Gables with the messuage 'with courtyard barn and a certain structure called a heyhowse & le gatehowse & gateway' sold by Andrew Loosely to James Henn, Senr. in 1631,[14] particularly when one reads its description when sold in 1869, 'a dwelling-house … adjoining is a Gateway entrance with capital Corn Loft over, an excellent yard, well-paved' etc.

The Market House, or at least its brick core, would have been familiar to Mrs. Chibnall. It will be discussed in greater detail in Chapter Four. In the High Street most buildings are Georgian or later although many replace or conceal earlier structures. The present-day *George & Dragon*, for example, had a predecessor which was already ancient in 1678. Not until Bell Street, the extremity of the town in Mrs. Chibnall's day, would she find the next familiar feature, the thatched cottage, no.28. It remains much as it was, several of its neighbours having been rebuilt or modified by the Baptists in the early 18th century.

By the beginning of the 19th century the two manors surrounding St Mary's Church, which had dominated the life of the town, were settling into a peaceful backwater and the modern town prepared to take the stage.

32 No.28 Bell Street, *c*.1920.

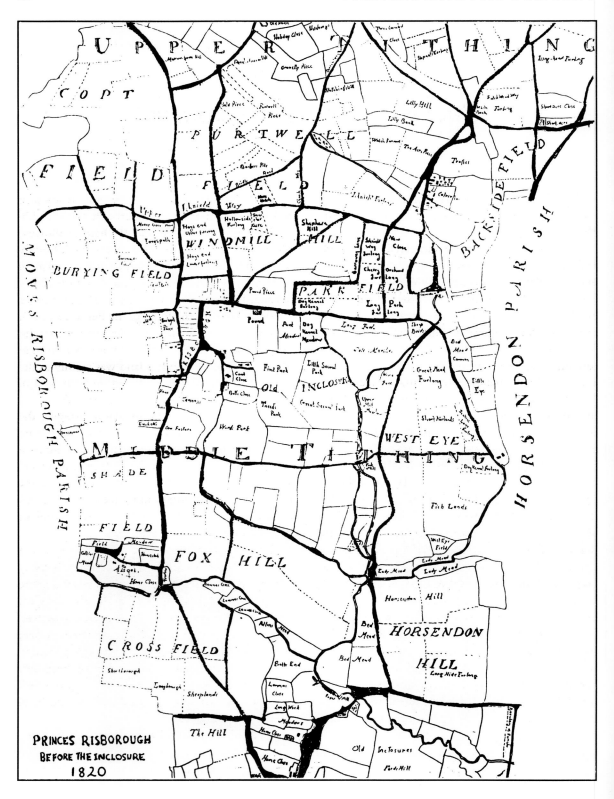

PRINCES RISBOROUGH
BEFORE THE INCLOSURE
1820

Chapter Three

Enclosure and Development

A T THE BEGINNING of the 19th century Princes Risborough presented itself, superficially at least, as a self-sufficient community. The population numbered about 1,200 and the economy was largely agricultural. Three-quarters of the workforce were employed on the land and most of the remainder provided services as butchers, bakers, grocers, tailors, shoemakers, smiths and so on. Manufacture was limited to the cottage production of such things as lace, straw hats, parchment and furniture for local use and there were a few small-scale maltsters supplying the alehouses.

However, all was not as well as it seemed and the collapse of the tower of St Mary's Church in 1804 might be seen as an omen of the serious problems that were beginning to arise. The end of the Napoleonic Wars led to a fall in the price of grain and farmers were forced to lay off workers, aggravating a national problem of unemployment due to the Industrial Revolution. In nearby High Wycombe anger was vented in rioting and the destruction of new machinery in its paper mills. The population was increasing and daily the poor became poorer and the cost of supporting them greater.

About a third of the acreage of the parish was in old enclosures, notably in the old royal park which had been set apart from the manor by Henry VIII, and in Longwick. The remainder was in open fields, with common land much as Nathaniel Anderson had described it a hundred years before as being mostly in the Chiltern part and overrun with shrubs of beech, while the pasturage belonged to a handful of the rich.[1, 2]

In 1819 three figures were prominent amongst the landowners in Princes Risborough; John Grubb, Lord George Cavendish and Richard Holloway. John Grubb lived at Horsenden Manor but his family had bought the manors of Risborough and part of the Penton estate in 1762. George Augustus Henry Cavendish (later Earl of Burlington) had bought 1,560 acres of the remainder of the Penton estate in 1813 from Thomas Grace, an Aylesbury banker who had purchased it earlier but was himself bankrupt in 1817.[3] Richard Holloway's land was mainly in the Lower Hamlet, from Ilmer Road up both sides of Longwick Road to the Lower Icknield Way.

These three were instrumental in bringing the necessary Bill before Parliament to allow enclosure of the open fields, arguing that it would improve productivity and bring a further 500 acres of 'waste' into cultivation, and that this would improve the pauper's lot by lowering food prices. It would also dispose of the vexed question of tithes, land or money being awarded in lieu.[4]

There was considerable opposition to the proposal, from small farmers already heavily mortgaged who, unable to bear the cost, would be forced to sell and join the ranks of the unemployed, and from those who, if not threatened themselves, saw the potential for disaster for their poorer neighbours.[5] In neighbouring Bledlow, enclosed in 1812, 'the agricultural labourer who had been able to supplement his income, however sparsely, was left a labourer without any land and any means of earning extra income'.[6]

Gradually the opposition was won over until a sufficient majority, at least in terms of acreage and Land Tax assessments, was obtained and the Bill

33 *(facing page)* Princes Risborough town and the Middle Tithing field system prior to enclosure in 1820.

34   *A Farmyard near Princes Risborough*, Samuel Palmer (1805–81). Samuel Palmer spent some time at Collins Farm, Loosley Row, and this watercolour in his early style was painted there. The pastoral scene, with Bledlow Cop in the background, typifies the agricultural community of Risborough prior to enclosure. (Victoria and Albert Museum)

received Royal Assent on 22 June 1820. It took nearly three years for the Commissioners to complete the necessary work (which included fencing, roadmaking and bridge building) to allow them to execute their Award and a further 18 months to settle all the accounts.[7]

The results of enclosure were much as predicted. John Grubb and Lord George both did extremely well while, at the opposite end of the scale, Martha East, a harness-maker living in the Market Square and one of a long-established local family, had her modest holding of about three roods, 14 poles reduced to 38 poles (i.e. four-fifths of an acre to less than a quarter acre). Many of the poor now became destitute and the Vestry was hard put to find ways of controlling the soaring Poor Rate.[8]

One solution was to oblige landowners to employ a minimum number of men or boys according to their land acreage and on the same basis assess them for a 'labour rate' which they could reduce by employing more of the 'surplus labour'. Minimum wages were established on a scale ranging from 8s. for men above 20 years of age down to 2s. a week for 10 to 12-year-old boys. In this way 196 men and boys were 'kept off the Parish' which nevertheless supported 140 able-bodied men and their families as paupers in 1835.

Some families followed their Bledlow neighbours to the Lancashire cotton mills under schemes set up by the Poor Law Commissioners who also fostered emigration to the colonies. Census Returns give some indication of the overall effect on the parish. In the second decade of the century the population rose by a little over 19 per cent from 1,644 to 1,958. In the 10 years after enclosure the increase fell dramatically to 8.4 per cent and only

35 An equally pastoral scene with the infant Owen Barnard, b.1889, in his grandmother's arms and his brother William in his perambulator, at the stile leading to Love's Path off Brimmer's Road, now New Road Hill.

managed an average 5 per cent per decade until 1871 when the population was 2,549.

Overall, despite the dire straits of the poor, Victorian Risborough moved rapidly towards greater prosperity and better education. One factor may have been the influence of two new major landowners. Nathan Mayer Rothschild came to England in 1798 and his son, Mayer Amschel, acquired much of Lord George Cavendish's land. Later the family were advised to concentrate their land holdings[9] and in 1858 Mayer Amschel exchanged land roughly corresponding to Culverton and Brimmers Farms for land belonging to Merton College, Oxford, in Cheddington, adding it to his park at Mentmore.[10]

Merton College had bought the 1,420-acre Wardrobes Farm from Charles Compton Cavendish in 1856 (at just under £12 an acre) and was a major landholder until 1945-6 when all its property in

the area was sold, mostly to local farmers. Among other benefits, the college made land available for allotments and a new rectory and the Rothschilds built the Literary Institute as a gift in 1891. They also bought and restored the much-delapidated Manor House in the 1880s, and the widow and family of Nathan's great-grandson, Charles, presented it to the National Trust in 1925.

Improved communications gave a further boost to the economy. Canals and railways were augmenting the turnpike roads. Plans for a canal across Aylesbury Vale came to nothing but in 1862 the Great Western Railway line from London via Maidenhead to High Wycombe was extended to Risborough and Thame. This provided a stimulus to development, particularly from Bell Street into Parkfield which until 1850 had been no more than a few scattered houses. In 1865 the landlord of the

36   The High Street, *c.*1885. The Misses Barnard, on the left, had a lace and millinery shop. Beyond the White House, home to members of the Stratton family, is a smaller house, demolished in 1891 to make way for the Rothschild Literary Institute.

37   In the 1930s George Jacobs, related to the Barnards and a one-time blacksmith, is established as a cycle and motor engineer and the White House now has a taller neighbour, the Literary Institute.

Bird in Hand applied (unsuccessfully) for his licence to be extended to include wine, since 38 cottages had been newly built near his premises.

Building plots were advertised, such as one in *The Bucks Advertiser* on 15 May 1869: 'situate at the South End and close to the Town [with] very extensive frontages to the Main Road … to the Station'. This became Warren's Row, 14-24 Wycombe Road, completed in 1878. That advertisement also gives a glimpse of a Victorian household as the property had lately belonged to Thomas Warren, surgeon, who had moved into the recently vacated 'vicarage' in the Market Square and was selling his house next to the *White Hart* in the High Street. On the ground floor, in addition to his surgery, were the hall, dining room, and a drawing room opening onto a very large 'pleasure garden'. On the first floor, another drawing room and the six principal bedrooms with four more on the second floor and, at the back, the scullery, kitchen and cellar, a coach house, two stables and 'other necessary outbuildings'. Its new owners, a family called Philps, were also the last, as it was demolished in the 1950s to make way for shops.

LORD ROTHSCHILD'S TENANTS.

WEDNESDAY, 14th MAY, 1890.

LUNCHEON TICKET.

Crown Hotel, Aylesbury,

AT 2.30.

38 The Rothschilds were concerned for the welfare of the community and their tenants. An invitation to Leonard Pauling, whose father took the lease of Red House Farm, Longwick, for him in 1879.

39 Leonard Pauling was born in this cottage at Monks Risborough, on what was then called the Coach Road, now Burton Lane. He was a gifted photographer and must have known Henry Taunt who took this picture. In 1902 he emigrated with his family to Whau Creek, Henderson, New Zealand, where his photographic collection is preserved.

Monks Risborough.

40 On the extreme right is the house of Mr. Thomas Warren, a surgeon, which he sold in 1869 to a widow, Mrs. Philps, whose family retained it for nearly 100 years. It was demolished and replaced by a Co-operative Society supermarket in the 1960s.

41 On the left of the Market Square is the former 'vicarage' into which Thomas Warren moved when the Wycombe Road rectory was built in 1865. It remained a doctor's house until the 1930s when Dr. Francis Cooper moved to Parkfield. His son, Dudley, later joined the much-respected Dr. Gwyn Edwards who was for many years Chairman of the Parish Council, at the *Cross Keys*.

42 Wycombe Road, looking towards Bell Street in the late 19th century. On the left is Warren's Row, built in 1878, facing allotments on which the Bell Street school was built in 1913.

Gas lighting was a welcome innovation. The *Thame Gazette* reported a dinner to celebrate the introduction of gas into the town on 9 August 1865. 'About 9 o'clock the inhabitants were astonished by the lighting of a brilliant star with gas in front of the George Hotel. Almost all the inhabitants turned out to see a sight … never witnessed before and they hope by the coming winter they may not have to walk in darkness any longer.' Previously there had been lamps burning naphtha, distilled from coal or wood tar, inefficient and foul-smelling. Unfortunately, despite the townsfolk's appreciation, the company and Vestry were constantly at loggerheads over costs, maintenance and lamplighting, a struggle continued by the Vestry's successor, the Parish Council, until the Risborough Gas & Coal Company was taken over by its Aylesbury rival in 1925 and the opportunity was taken to switch to electricity.

43 Gas comes to Risborough. The Methodist chapel account January to March 1877.

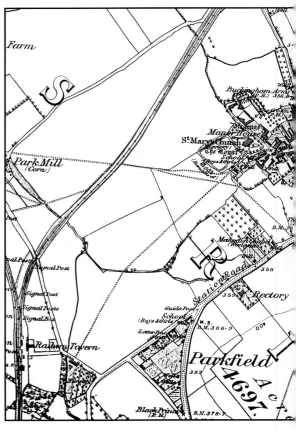

44 *(above)*   A well uncovered in 1996 during work on the
Tesco site. It had a flint lining, capped with brick but contained
nothing more interesting than a sheep's thigh bone.

45 *(above right)*   The junction of Longwick Road and Duke
Street in the 1930s, almost unrecognisable today with the
roadworks consequent on the new Tesco superstore. The well,
previously illustrated, was under the long-vanished Olde Blue
Kettle teashop at the right hand end of Duke Street.

46 *(below right)*   Princes Risborough as surveyed in 1877 for
the Ordnance Survey published 1885.

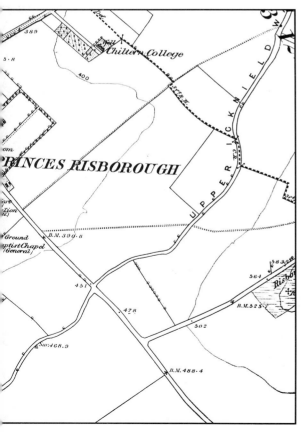

In September 1898 a severe drought caused great distress and £5 a week was voted by the Parish Council towards supplying needy cases. The town itself had good wells, so this was mainly a problem in the Upper Hamlets where most of the water came from ponds such as the three in Lacey Green reserved for drinking. Precious though they were, there are numerous references in council minutes to abuse, and as late as 1913 the District Council had to put up notices saying ducks and cattle were prohibited from going into them! One might have thought that a good water supply would have been a greater priority than gas or electricity but it came later than both, in 1926.

From the stormy beginning of the 19th century to the Great War of 1914-18 there had been greater change than in any previous century. Sixty-four names from that conflict are recorded on the memorial tablet under the Market House but those who returned were better able to take charge of their future than any before.

Chapter 4

Charters, Fairs and Markets

IN 1523, 'at the humble supplication of our tenants and inhabitants of our town of Prynserisburgh', Henry VIII granted a weekly Wednesday market and two annual fairs, the first to be held on the eve, day and morrow of the Nativity of the Blessed Virgin Mary (7-9 September) and the other on the eve, day and morrow of St George the Martyr (22-24 April) for the improvement of the status of the town and its inhabitants.

Although the King enjoined his heirs that the market and fairs should be held unless they were to the prejudice of others in the neighbourhood, the fairs have come under threat on the grounds of general nuisance. In 1895 Samuel Adcock proposed that the recently-formed Parish Council 'do away with them' and the Clerk wrote to both District and County Councils to enlist their support, which was unforthcoming. The District Council said that 'a Memorial from the Inhabitants … that they desire the removal of these fairs should have accompanied the letter' and the County Council asked to be

informed 'under what Act of Parliament … it is suggested that [they] can take any steps in the matter'. Since the Parish Council was unlikely to obtain the former and did not know the answer to the latter the magistrates were approached but said 'they were powerless to act in the matter as it was in the hands of the District Council'.

It is easy to be critical of those early assaults, forgetting what the Market Square was like before the roads were modernised. Thomas Parsons, speaking of the 1830s, said that 'on a market day, it was necessary because the road was so very bad, to strew around the market house a quantity of straw to protect the people from going knee-deep in mud … there were only two or three places in the street by which they could pass, owing to the deep ruts in the road'. A less justifiable objection is the impediment to modern traffic flow.

The Agricultural Association's shows at Culverton Farm, regularly reported in *The Times* but which ended with the Second World War,

47 Pettigrove's 'Golden, galloping horses', with the brewery arch and lion behind.

48 The Market House in 1910 with all its arches open and ladder to the upper storey.

probably more closely resembled the original fairs than do those of today. The latter are now held on 5-7 May and 20-22 October. They are shadows of their former selves but no less enjoyable for that, with Pettigrove's 'golden, galloping horses' in the square and side shows in Church Street.

The Market House is a reminder of the lapsed weekly market although what appears today is the result of several interventions which, however practical, obscure the simple lines of the original. It is thought to date from the mid-17th century when its Flemish bond brick-work, with alternating 'headers' and 'stretchers' on every row, was competing with earlier decorative styles of which another, 'herringbone', once graced its neighbour, The Gables. The building comprised eight arches embracing an open area and supporting an upper room which was formerly a grain store, reached by a ladder, but is now the Town Council chamber with an enclosed staircase.

In 1824 John Grubb, whose great-uncle John had acquired the manor in 1762, restored the building, perhaps in recognition of the benefits

49 The Market House in 1996 showing the closure of the rear arches and, below the window, the outline of the bricked-up door which so troubled Thomas Wright.

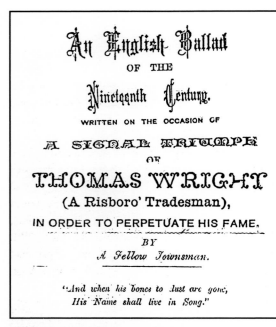

An English Ballad
OF THE
Nineteenth Century.
WRITTEN ON THE OCCASION OF
A SIGNAL TRIUMPH
OF
THOMAS WRIGHT
(A Risboro' Tradesman),
IN ORDER TO PERPETUATE HIS FAME.

BY
A Fellow Townsman.

"And when his bones to dust are gone,
His Name shall live in Song."

52 Thomas Wright's 'triumph' was to be invited to sing for the Earl of Buckingham at Hampden House.

51 *(right)* The title page of a copy of the Risborough Charter and *(far right)* the reference to non-molestation of residents of Risborough

enclosure had brought him. He added a slated 'skirt' to extend the covered ground area and a cupola to house a clock bought by public subscription (the church tower clock having not been replaced after the collapse of the tower in 1804). This clock was itself replaced by one with four faces when further restoration was undertaken in 1920 as part of the memorial to those who fell in the First World War and whose names are recorded under the eaves.

The building was a constant source of friction and a drain on the parish purse. Thomas Wright, 'a tradesman of repute, who in the Decorative Art excels beyond dispute',[1] complained that his business next door to what is now Lloyds Bank was obstructed by carts parked in the narrow gap as they

A Copy of the Charter Granted to the Inhabitants of Princes Risborough in the year 1598

To All Christian People To whome these Presents shall Come I Sir Edward Knollys Knt. Controller of our Lady the Queens Houshold and one of her Majestys most honourable Privy Council And alsoe Constable of the Castle and Manner of Wallingford and Head Steward of the Honour of Wallingford

delivered grain. He also resisted the re-opening of the old loft doors whose outline can still be discerned in the wall facing the bank.

In 1888, when the Vestry sought to demolish the building, there was a long-running dispute over ownership. Mr. Sulston, who worked the Manor Farm, was the tenant and refused to give it up, claiming old rights. John Grubb's son said that his father had intended it to pass to the parish after his restoration and the Rothschilds' solicitors, Horwood and James, wrote '… we cannot without perusing the documents of title speak … with certainty but as you contemplate removal of the building as part of your intended improvement of the town we have no doubt Lord Rothschild will … concur in any action to that end'.[2]

Moderating its plans, the Vestry considered selling the 'shedding' to pay for repairs but settled for the offer of the balance of Queen Victoria's Jubilee Fund. Both the Vestry and Wright almost had their problems resolved in 1901 by a steamroller which struck a corner of the building. The building, symbol of the past, now seems safe within the town conservation area.

A leather-bound document purporting to be a 'Copy of the Charter granted to the Inhabitants of Princes Risborough in the year 1598' is in the author's possession. It is undated but the 'laid' paper (watermarked Britannia and countermarked GR), the ink and handwriting suggest the early 18th century and Lipscomb records a copy which had been endorsed by successive Sheriffs, the last on

16 July 1713.[3] It recites various grants first made by Henry I, enlarged and ratified by Henry II and III, and now being confirmed on behalf of Elizabeth I by Sir Edward Knollys, Constable of the castle and manor of Wallingford and a Privy Councillor.

It affords liegemen and merchants of Berkhampstead and Wallingford (which included Risborough) freedom of travel on business 'throughout all our dominions of England and Normandy Aquitania and Andigavia [Anjou] By Water and by Land, by Wood and by Strand' and excuses them all manner of taxes and restraints, 'toll, passage, pontage, piccage and stallage' to name but a few. They are also excused various duties including jury service, but unfortunately this privilege is no longer accepted by the Courts!

It is a reminder of the links between England and France from the Norman Conquest through the Plantagenet dynasty, being addressed to all subjects 'as well France as Inglish' and effective in seaports 'this side the sea and on the other side'. Of particular local interest is a specific injunction from Elizabeth I that all her subjects, of whatever Estate, 'do wholly forbeare to demand or receive any thing of Thos Bowler of Longwick, Thos Bowler of Culverton Thos Wade John Wade Edward Hawse John Dorsett William Neale Henery Claydon Edmund Clinkard Ralph Hawse and all others ... Tennants and Residence of the Manner of Princes Risborough'.

The copyist's spelling is at times idiosyncratic and at one point he causes confusion by writing 'Henery the fifth' for 'Henery the first'. However, it seems clear that those named had been aggrieved in some way and had joined together to sue for their rights. Their family names appear many times over the years though alternative spellings are common: for example, Bowler or Boller, Dorsett or Dossett, Clinkard or Clinkett, and some are still to be found in the town.

The two royal 'charters' carry little or no statutory weight today but they, and the families who earned them, are valued as evidence of a proud past.

Chapter Five

Church and Chapel

S T MARY'S CHURCH is first mentioned in the 12th century, as part of the endowment of Notley Abbey on the river Thame below Long Crendon. However, the earliest elements seen today are the eight magnificent octagonal pillars framing the nave which date from about 1250 when the church was enlarged by the addition of north and south aisles and the raising of a clerestory. Soon after that the church was extended westwards, supported by pillars of a different style. The beautiful south window with its supporting columns is from this period, together with some other masonry. A tower was built, or perhaps rebuilt, in the 15th century.

It is easy to think of such solid medieval edifices as enduring for ever, but such was certainly not the case. The registers of 1550 record the sale of 'A chalice, a sensurre and ij pyxes of sylver by consent of the whole parish for covering the church'. In 1637, when the church was in the diocese of

52   St Mary's Church, drawn by J. Buckler in 1837. Note the porch, tower and spire, the rectangular clerestory and east windows and low-pitched roof. (Bodleian Library, MS. Top. Bucks. a.1, fol 8r)

53   St Mary's in 1890, after Arthur Blomfield's restoration. The east window is now in Perpendicular style, the roof having been lifted, the clerestory windows are now roundels and the porch has a gabled roof.

54   'Tomlinson of Thame made me 1783' but there was no place for the old turret clock in the 1907 spire and it sits forlornly in the belfry.

Lincoln,[1] the archdeacon made a general visitation of churches in the county and St Mary's, like many others, was found to be in a general state of decay in its stone and woodwork. In particular, mention was made of 'the top of the steeple leading up to the Leads in decay'.

The term 'steeple' can cause confusion. *Chambers Dictionary* defines it as 'a church or other tower, with or without, or including or excluding, a spire; a structure surmounted by a spire: the spire alone'! A letter from the curate, Nathaniel Anderson,[2] c.1715, to the antiquarian Browne Willis, makes it clear that St Mary's had a tower.

Pride, they say, comes before a fall. A new clock bearing the proud inscription 'Risborough clock I be Tomlinson of Thame made me 1783' was installed in the tower, replacing an older one. Disaster struck on 1 February 1804 when a note at the end of the Burial Register for 1786-1812 baldly states that the 'tower fell down'. In a letter to the archdeacon the writer says that the bells and lead had been taken out of the ruins and asks for advice but a fortnight later is still awaiting a reply though able to report the church 'fit for Divine Service as of Sunday last'.[3]

Five great bells and a saint's bell had been mentioned as early as 1552 and Anderson also mentions them. They were sold to the Whitechapel Bell Foundry where the two bells that hang today were cast, a small one dated 1805 from the old metal and another dated 1861, dedicated to J. Lovegrove Norris, a former surgeon, by his widow Sarah.

The tower was rebuilt, this time with a spire and maybe too hastily for in 1826 the 'steple' is reported as 'built with any kind of timber, Deal, Ash & Elm ... let the wet in for 15-20 years'. Henry Crook tendered to repair the spire, tower, ceiling and make a new pair of doors for £154 11s., the spire to be of 'best Yellow Christiana battens with two octagonal curbs ... boarding of Memel Fir. Ball and base to be covered in lead, ball painted yellow ... whole of external spire to be painted with anti-chorrosion Stone colour'.[4] Although not specifically mentioned, zinc sheeting covered the boarding and the paint was good enough to deceive Lipscomb[5] into thinking the spire was of stone.

In 1842 the churchyard was enlarged southwards by some 37ft. and the boundary wall erected after closure of the adjacent workhouse and conveyance of 'part of a site of certain cottages called the Church Houses'.[6] Then, in the 1860s, the architect Arthur Blomfield (later knighted) undertook a major restoration which included raising the roof and enlarging the east window in the chancel while replacing the old clerestory

55 Neither the Lovegrove Norris bell, on the left, nor the saint's bell, can safely be rung today.

windows with smaller roundels. Modernisation was completed in 1907 when the old tower and spire, 'the most unsightly in England ... of indescribably rusty appearance'[7] were replaced to the design of John Oldrid Scott, son of George Gilbert Scott who had himself modernised St Mary's, Aylesbury, and was great-grandson of the Rev. Thomas Scott of Aston Sandford.

An indenture of 1586 refers to 'all the Rectory ... sometyme belonging ... unto the late dissolved monastery of Notley'[8] and shows that patronage of the living had come into lay hands where it remained

56 St Mary's just after the modern 'pork pie and marmalade' spire was raised in 1907. It acquired the nickname from the fund-raising stalls organised by the rector's daughter. (Ronald Goodearl)

The Vicarage, Princes Risborough. 10795

57   The Wycombe Road rectory, built in 1865 and demolished almost 100 years later.

until 1860 when it passed to the Bishop of Oxford and in 1975 to the Lord Chancellor. It was technically a Curacy or later a 'Perpetual' Curacy and was not formally elevated to a Rectory until 1868.

Although the old house now called Monk's Staithe, to the north-east of the churchyard, is reputed to have had associations with Notley Abbey and was formerly known as the Old Vicarage, the first 'official residence' that can be identified with certainty is the fine square house at the north-west corner of the Market Square. It was bought by the church at the behest of Richard Meade, incumbent from 1811-44, as there was 'no house belonging to the Benefice'[9] and his two immediate predecessors had lived there prior to its last occupant, Richard Darvill, who had been adjudged bankrupt. Funds came from Queen Anne's Bounty, set up to help the poorer clergy by restoring tithes which Henry VIII had taken for his own use.

By 1865 this house was no longer considered adequate for the administrative needs of the living and a new one was built,[10] half a mile from the town centre in the Wycombe Road on an acre of ground given by Merton College, Oxford. This was replaced by a more modest house opposite the church in 1954. The 1865 rectory was demolished and replaced by Icknield Court, a residential home for the elderly, a function now also served by the 1954 rectory which became an Abbeyfield House in 1987, the rectory moving to Manor Park Avenue.

The Baptist church was established by the mid-17th century, meeting in members' houses. The building itself was founded in 1707 when Jane Cork and her son William granted John Coker and others a lease for 980 years at an annual peppercorn rent on 'all that parcel of ground … being part of the orchard belonging to the cottage wherein John Wolled did dwell … to erect a meeting house for Protestant Dissenters now called Peculiar Baptists'.

In 1726 Thomas Cartwright, a papermaker of Loosley Row who was to become a major benefactor of the church, acquired adjoining properties

58   The Baptist Church or 'Upper Meeting', *c.*1900.

in what is now Bell Street, including John Wolled's cottage, and made cottages and land over to the church on his death in 1745. Wolled's cottage was rebuilt and eventually amalgamated with Thomas Cartwright's own cottage, remaining as the church manse until sold for commercial use in 1958.

The church building itself was enlarged in 1804 and again in 1814, from 18 x 32ft. to 49ft. square. In 1817 a Sunday School started and for 'the promised dinner' given to the children on New Year's Eve 92lbs. of beef, 12 gallons of beer, salt, potatoes, plums and currants, spices and lard, bread and flour and a new baking dish were purchased for a total of £4 12s. 10½d. What a feast!

Between 1870 and 1890 a group separated from the parent church, calling themselves the Free Baptists and worshipping at the 'iron' church on land donated by brewer Thomas Parsons. When they re-united, this building reverted to the brewery and was used for social events. It was bought by William Chalfont, the brewery manager, and for a

time was known as the Chalfont Hall. Today it is the Walsingham Hall, belonging to the Catholic church. The full-immersion baptismal font is said to remain under the stage.

The various religious communities seem to have lived in harmony over the centuries in Risborough, even to the extent of sharing their buildings, but the history of other nonconformist groups in the town is very difficult to elucidate for lack of written records. Confusion arises with the appearance of an independent church in the 17th century. George Swinho, who had been ejected from St Leonards, near Wendover, led a 'private congregation' in Princes Risborough and the record of his burial on 27 November 1704 describes him as 'a presbiterian minister'.

His church was a square red-brick building with a gallery, in Back Lane behind the *George*, and had links with both the Baptists and Methodists. When the Baptist church or 'upper meeting' was being altered in 1804 members were allowed to use the

38 PRINCES RISBOROUGH PAST

59 The Methodist church with its original façade.

Back Lane building or 'lower meeting'. Sheehan, writing in 1869,[11] says that the church then remained empty for some fifty years until bought by the Wesleyan Methodists, the Presbyterians having 'disappeared'. *Musson and Craven's Directory* of 1853 identifies it as the church of the Wesleyan Methodists who later decided it was 'inconveniently situated' and built the present church in the Wycombe Road in 1869. Perhaps its proximity to the *George* conflicted with Methodist temperance. The building was subsequently used as assembly rooms and, during the Second World War, as the headquarters of the local Home Guard. It was demolished in the late 1950s and unfortunately no picture of it is known other than aerial views showing its unusual triple-ridge roof.

The Methodist church stands on a narrow plot, too small for its needs, 'whether by lack of foresight, faith, funds or a combination of all three' wrote one of the congregation perhaps frustrated by the restrictions this imposed on its ministry. The original façade was hidden behind a new facing in the 1970s when a lobby was also added. Its membership, small in numbers but not in faith, is actively seeking a better solution.

The first Roman Catholic Mass to be said in Princes Risborough since the Reformation was in 1923, in the previously mentioned Chalfont Hall, and from 1924 until 1970 Catholics from far afield shared in a Whitsun procession culminating in a sermon in the Market Square.

The present church, dedicated to St Teresa of the Child Jesus, sprang from humble origins in an army hut brought from Halton in 1927 and converted into a chapel in the Longwick Road on the site now occupied by the bungalow called 'Shrove Furlong', itself named after a farm in Kingsey. In 1937 work began on the Modern ('jazz-modern' wrote Sir John Betjeman and John Piper)[12] Byzantine church whose form, to the design of Giuseppe Rinvolucri, is said to represent a rose, emblem of St Teresa. By 1960 the exterior needed repair, on completion of which a cross was placed on the dome. In 1974, largely for acoustic reasons, the altar was re-positioned at the west end with a new porch at the east.

Directly and indirectly the churches not only provide for the spiritual needs of their congregations but, as is fitting, also contribute to the educational, recreational and welfare needs of the whole community.

60 St Teresa's Church with its presbytery, both buildings innovatively designed.
61 The procession to the opening ceremony of St Teresa's Roman Catholic Church in 1937. (Goodearl)

Chapter Six

Law and Order

FORMER INHABITANTS of Princes Risborough, like their modern counterparts, seem mostly to have been law-abiding. Local records show little evidence of serious crime or major public disturbance. This was just as well, particularly where repeated offending was concerned, in the face of penalties more severe than the recent American 'three hits and you're out'. In 1352, for instance, a Cheshire miner stealing ore faced a fine for the first offence, doubled for a second but for a third 'his right hand shall be pierced with a knife through the palm and pinned … [up] to the handle of the knife, and so he shall stay … until he be dead or get his hand free'.[1]

From the Norman era to the mid-19th century the people were supervised by officers elected annually by the Manor Court Jury or later by the Select Vestry. There were two types of manor court, the Court Leet which dealt mainly with law and order, and the Court Baron for matters affecting property and tenure. The jury was usually made up of 12 men accepted as knowing the obligations and rights of both lord and tenants.

In Princes Risborough two Petty Constables were normally elected, one for the town and one for the parish. The Upper Hamlets of Loosley Row, Lacey Green and Speen also had their own Headborough, sometimes called tithing-man or Abbot's constable, Speen in particular having been part of the Abbot's manor. The officers were unpaid but could claim their expenses and were responsible, with the High Constable of the Hundred, to the Justices at Quarter Sessions.

Constables could command the assistance of inhabitants in maintaining law and order as watchmen though they could not necessarily depend on getting it. In January 1696, for instance, John Darvill of Darval's Hill in Speen was presented to the Justices for refusing to keep watch when called on by the constable.[2] If there was serious unrest order could be enforced by the army or one of the two civilian elements of the armed forces. These were the Militia, raised from property owners by compulsory ballot and the Yeomanry, created in 1794.

Among constabulary duties was the collection of certain rates including that for the County Militia. In 1685, for example, £5 19s. 6d. was raised and £5 17s. 6d. laid out for pay, powder, bullets, new arms, new bandoliers, etc. A more pleasant task was the organisation of local celebrations such as bonfires on 'Gunpowder treason night'. In 1690 the constables paid 3s. 0d. to the bellringers 'when the King came from Ireland'. This was William III, of Orange, husband of Mary. His bloodless intervention in 1688 against the Catholic James II confirmed England's Protestantism and led to a parliamentary Declaration of Rights which established the first modern Constitutional Monarchy.

Although not strictly speaking democratic, the Declaration represented the views of the majority of the nobility, land-owners and merchants who, as vestry records, etc. show us, effectively shaped the lives of the people, in Risborough as elsewhere. Of course, not everyone was happy. At the Michaelmas Quarter Sessions of 1690 Ralph Lacey was indicted for keeping a disorderly alehouse and speaking seditious words about the King and Queen but took the required oath of allegiance. His alehouse was suppressed and he was fined a total of £5 3s. 4d.[3]

Constables were required to present themselves to the Justices at Quarter Sessions where amongst other things they reported on roads, alehouses and matters of general complaint and public well-being. For example, in 1678 the inhabitants of Princes Risborough were indicted for not repairing Pound Lane (the pound was near the site of the present British Legion Hall) and Daniel Aldridge was 'licenced to sell beer and ale in the Ancient Alehouse called The George' while in 1805 it was said that 'a well on premises belonging to Mrs. Child lies open to the public and they are endangered'.

Early in the 19th century the Chairman of Quarter Sessions noted the prevalence of assaults on constables and some of the Risborough constable's remarks imply an upsurge of unruly behaviour. In 1823 he suggested that 'a cage for temporary confinement would be useful, there formerly was one'. The *Bird Cage* inn at Thame is said to have had such a cage outside for use on market days. Over the next few years the constable also protested 'the stocks are not yet fixed up … the stocks are out of the ground' and in 1827 laid the

62 *(top)*   The stocks at Dinton.

63 *(above)*   The so-called 'Risborough stocks'.

ultimate complaint 'no stocks' adding that 'the Lord of the Manor usually has repaired them'. He was speaking of something first raised two hundred years earlier, at the Court Baron of Joan Chibnall held on 24 April 1626, when it had been said that 'le stocks and le pound are ruinous'. The stocks were

64   Children pose outside the first police station, those 'new-looking cottages' of the Foreword, in Station Road, c.1905.

important to him as almost the only sanction he could apply at his own discretion, used in their latter years mainly for the suppression of drunkenness.

The Horsenden constable might be credited with originating the 'stock answer' when in the early 19th century he attended every Quarter Sessions simply to state 'No Stocks'. He had little enough else to occupy him; no significant offence had been committed on his 'patch' since an early breach of planning regulations in 1695 when Richard Saunders enclosed part of the highway at Horsenden by making a hedge and ditch at a place called North Piece and the sheriff was ordered to 'totally remove the said nuisance'.

It is not known where the stocks stood in Princes Risborough but it seems probable that they were near the church, like those still standing in nearby Dinton. They have one end post furnished with iron shackles similar to some labelled 'Risborough Stocks' (though without any supporting evidence) which were found some years ago in a London antique shop. This formed the whipping post where offenders, more often than

not the least capable and perhaps the least culpable, were dealt with for offences such as theft, vagrancy and giving birth out of wedlock.

In the latter respect those who sheltered mothers of illegitimate children might be called to account before the Justices or the Archdeaconry Court, though not dealt with so cruelly. When William Phillipe was convicted at Risborough on 28 May 1606 'for keeping in his house a woman who was great with child and for suffering her to depart unexamined and without punishment', he had himself to perform a public penance at Morning Prayer in his parish church where with 'a white sheet wound about him from ye shoulders to ye anckles, and a white rod in his hand, bare legged and bare footed, ... standing uppe in some open space where he maie well be seen of the congregation, shall saie ... I am nowe come hither to acknowledge such my fault ...'.[4] Fathers were pursued only insofar as was necessary to prevent any expense falling on the parish.

An example of unruly behaviour, taken from papers of the Ayres' family who had a farm in the

High Street, was a disturbance in 1819. John Hester, governor of the workhouse, Thomas Ayres the younger, farmer, John Ayres, tailor, John Smith and Joseph Tolland, labourers, were accused of riot and assault on one Henry Hatton. Much to the annoyance of the Ayres' solicitor (already irritated by his clients' failure to keep appointments), two of the others determined to plead guilty, therefore all pleaded guilty at the Epiphany Sessions. The fines imposed show some sense of social justice; John Hester £2, each of the Ayres £1, Smith and Tollard 1s. (*Pigot's Directory* of 1823 lists a John Hester, brewer and maltster and Thomas Ayres, tailor and draper.)

The Rural Constabulary Act of 1839 sealed the fate of the old petty constable.[5] The constable's task had become increasingly unpopular and, since the only way an eligible citizen could avoid his term was to provide a deputy, the post was often unsuitably filled. An increase in crime in large conurbations together with unrest associated with the industrial revolution encouraged a change to a paid force freed from the limitations of parochial boundaries though still under local jurisdiction.

The Act was initially discretionary and although there had been rioting in 1831 in High Wycombe over unemployment (as a result of which 19 people were sentenced to death, later commuted to trans-portation, imprisonment or fines), the Buckinghamshire Justices were reluctant to change, continuing to rely on parish constables until the compulsory County and Borough Police Act of 1856 led to the first paid police force in the county in 1857. In 1890 responsibility for the force became shared in a standing joint committee composed of equal numbers of justices and councillors.

The first police station in Princes Risborough was in the flint houses at the bottom of Station Road, but in 1925 it was moved to two houses in the Wycombe Road with the office between and later a reputedly bomb-proof garage to protect the precious police car, an Austin 7. In 1963 the present Longwick Road site was adopted. The modern-day equivalent of the auxiliary yeoman was the special constable who first appeared during a time of labour unrest before the First World War but quickly won an affectionate place in the community. One such in Risborough was the long-serving Baptist minister, the Rev. J. Neighbour.

In the 19th century Petty Sessions were held monthly at the *Cross Keys* or *George*. Baron Rothschild's gift to the town of the Literary Institute in 1891 provided a more formal venue though formality was sometimes strained by the lack of a retiring room for one of the two courtrooms. When the magistrates needed to deliberate in private the

65 In 1910, the days of horse and cart and bicycle 10 miles an hour was considered a proper maximum speed.

66   When the administration of justice was transferred from the congenial atmosphere of the *Cross Keys* or the *George* to the Literary Institute in 1891 it was just a small step across the road, but followed by a giant leap to Aylesbury in the 1980s.

accused, advocates, witnesses and friends were cleared from the court into the corridor, leading to much congestion and good-natured banter. A notable magistrate in those years was Mr. Stratfold Read of Saunderton, a farmer and county alderman. He served as chairman of the bench until he was 90 and at 93, with a distinguished colleague, Major James Caldwell of Speen, was applying his mind to the problem of how to deal with that product of the 20th century, the motoring offender.

The Risborough court was closed in 1980, having already merged with the Aylesbury bench in the relentless pursuit of efficiency. Until then Aylesbury sessions had been held in the County Court building but, also in 1980, a purpose-built magistrates' court was opened in Aylesbury by HRH The Princess Anne. Amalgamation was completed by the inclusion of Brill and Linslade benches and the centuries-old tradition of truly local justice came to an end.

Chapter Seven

Rich and Poor

IN HIS CLASSIC WORK *The Parish Chest*,[1] W.E. Tate has pointed out the intimate connection between the parish and the poor and how 'in the great days of parochial self-government the amount of time, attention and money spent on matters relating to the poor seems to have been quite as great as ... to all other matters of local concern together' and even in comparatively comfortable Risborough this was certainly the case.

Responsibility for the poor was divided between the manor and the church, the former by statute and the latter by obligation. In the 17th century two particularly significant Acts defined the role of the parish: that of Elizabeth I in 1601 which provided for the nomination of the churchwardens and two to four substantial householders as overseers of the poor, and that of Charles II in 1662 relating to settlement and removal.

The latter was an attempt to define which parish had ultimate responsibility for a pauper. Settlement was initially determined by birthplace (modified by parental rights) but could be acquired elsewhere, for example by serving as a parish officer or being gainfully employed for a year or more. Vestry and Quarter Sessions records of the 18th century are full of accounts of attempts to avoid responsibility for what was undoubtedly a growing problem, with human lives treated as pieces in the game.

Thus, in 1712, months of legal argument over the fate of 10-year-old Ann Taylor were resolved when it was determined that she had been born in Haddenham when her mother was a widowed vagrant. When her mother subsequently moved to Risborough and married 'one Somersby, a poor person whose rent was paid by the parish', Ann was above the age of nine years and her mother was deemed not to have acquired any rights in Risborough.

The justices appear to have tried to be considerate and were not above delivering a rap over the knuckles to the overseers. On more than one occasion costs were awarded against Risborough on the grounds of unduly obtained orders and 'frivolous, vexatious and groundless' appeals. In Monks Risborough similarly, the churchwardens and overseers were ordered to attend court over the case of Richard Dossett, 'a poor lame impotent person'. Over at least two years argument raged while he protested that 'his wife and children were starving and must inevitably perish if not relieved'.

The area around the parish church was of great importance to the poor in past times. Papers of the antiquarian Browne Willis in the Bodleian Library include a letter from Nathaniel Anderson, curate of Princes Risborough from 1709-21 in which he mentions 'many church houses adjoining to the churchyard ... kept in good repair for the use of the poor'.[2] They are referred to again in a document of 1839 recording the transfer of 'that piece or parcel of ground being part of a site of certain cottages called the Church Houses' which had become the site of the parish workhouse.

The workhouse had been built adjacent to the south side of the churchyard soon after the Act of 1723 which authorised the buying or renting of workhouses. It was a substantial 'brick and tiled building with out-offices and garden, partly enclosed by a wall and entered by a pair of close gates, one rood and four poles with a frontage towards the church 72ft. and a wing fronting the street of 62ft.

67   The now-demolished Wycombe Union workhouse at Saunderton, *c.*1900.

including the gateway access to cottages in occupations of Widow Charey, Elizabeth Bradwell and Mary Mines'.[3] Next to the site and once a parish officer's house, the present-day Corner Cottage has two bricks engraved with the date 1763.

In 1827 the workhouse comprised 'Governor's room, kitchen, front pantry, vestry room, back kitchen, bakehouse, old pantry, yard and garden, Governor's chamber, bacon room, men's room, women's room, Joshua Ward's room & room next to garden' at which time it accommodated eight boys, four men, five women (one with two children) and four other children.[4] Many elderly people ended their days in the workhouse, among them Henry Sinkfield, known as 'Sinful', who died there in 1816, aged 80, and John Saunders, 'for many years father of this Parish', who died in 1817, aged ninety-six.

Each year the Select Vestry, predecessor of the Parish Council, appointed a guardian who tendered for a salary from which he or she would maintain not only the residents but also a specified number of other townsfolk deemed to be in need but not requiring admission. The guardian was also responsible for the contents of the workhouse, including clothing, recorded by detailed inventories at the beginning and end of each appointment. In 1810 the valuation of the furniture and clothing was £60 8s. 6d.

Agreements for 'letting of the poor' provided additional income to help defray the cost of this support with provision for any excess to be paid to the paupers themselves. One such agreement details a contractual obligation on the part of the parish to buy stones picked under the guardian's order. However, at Quarter Sessions in 1830 the justices referred to the widespread and illegal practice of 'farming the labour of the poor for the private profit of a contractor'. (They also commented on the prevalent evil of young men marrying and immediately throwing themselves on the parish for relief!)

Poverty associated with the industrial revolution and land enclosure meant that by 1834 the administration of the poor had become so costly and problematic that the old parochial system was replaced by amalgamation into Unions. The Princes

68 On 3 September 1911 the Princes Risborough Mutual Benefit Society held a Church Parade, led by the Monks Risborough Brass Band, in support of the Royal Bucks Hospital.

69 The Buckingham Arms Slate Club XI, sometime before the First World War. It consisted mainly of members of the related Rogers and Rutland families with, second from the left in the back row, George Saw, bugler to the Fire Brigade and gardener to the Stratton family.

Risborough workhouse was sold to Richard White of Longwick for £241 0s. 0d. in 1839. With other assets a total of £664 5s. 0d. was realised. £100 was spent on a wall between the property and the churchyard but most of the proceeds were applied to establishing the Wycombe Union. The National School (now the parish hall) was built on part of the workhouse site while the Union was ultimately

70   The Risborough Juvenile Oddfellows Drum and Fife Band, *c.*1910, led by shoemaker Thomas Butler.

71   Timothy East was a Trustee of the Risborough Lodge of the Manchester Unity of the Independent Order of Oddfellows. Son of a harness maker, he was himself a fellmonger and coal merchant. He served as Guardian of the Poor, District Councillor, Manager of the British and Bell Street schools, and Lieutenant, Hon. Secretary and Treasurer of the Fire Brigade. He died in 1916 at the age of seventy.

housed at Slough near Saunderton in 11 acres of garden, serving 33 parishes with its own school on what had been its original site in Perry Lane, Bledlow. The Union building was ultimately demolished and the site is currently occupied by the pharmaceutical company, Janssen-Cilag.

Friendly Societies were another source of support, usually associated with an inn and raising funds

72   St Agatha's Waifs and Strays Girls Home, *c*.1920, with Clovellie, as it was then called, on its left and Whiteleaf Cross more clearly visible than today from the combined grazing of rabbits and sheep.

for the ill or bereaved. They became well-recognised as a social service by Parliament and relief for their funds was granted provided their rules were approved by Quarter Sessions. The first to be so approved in Bucks was the Benefit Club of the *Cross Keys*, dating from 1765. Two others followed, the *George* in 1843 and the *White Lion* in 1845, but it seems that in May 1863 these were all amalgamated into the Princes Risborough Mutual Benefit Society. That met at the *George* and for its lowest monthly contribution of 1s. 9d. provided 8s. per week with medical attendance. Less formal but as valuable were Slate Clubs, for example that of the *Buckingham Arms*.

The Manchester Unity of the Independent Order of Oddfellows formed a lodge in Princes Risborough in 1856, meeting at the *Wheatsheaf* and later, when that became the Capital and Counties Bank, at the Literary Institute. To encourage youngsters it had a Junior Fife and Drum Band.

Unfortunately, following administrative moves to Aylesbury and later to Leighton Buzzard, its records have not come to light.

The Church of England Children's Society opened a Waifs and Strays Girls Home in 1909. Much of the cost was met 'in memoriam' by the widow of the Rev. Bardolph, rector from 1895-7. The refuge later softened its name to the simpler St Agatha's Home, providing shelter for both boys and girls and, in 1996, was closed, seemingly lacking further purpose.

What is so striking in considering these matters is that, while much of the cruelty and disregard of human rights has disappeared from the care of the needy, those needs seem no less and society no better able to solve the underlying problems than four hundred years ago. Indeed, in some respects the wheel has turned full circle with conditions of residence and compulsory labour again featuring in welfare legislation.

Chapter Eight

Plague and Pestilence

PRIOR to the 16th century organised medical care throughout the land seems largely to have been in the hands of religious houses. Amongst the earliest references in Buckinghamshire is one quoted by Lipscomb,[1] that 'at an inquisition in 1360 it was stated that the hospitals of St Leonard and St John at Aylesbury were founded with the sanction and confirmation of Henry I and Henry II to sustain infirm lepers and other destitute persons'. The hospitals were already in decline then and neither site is known with certainty. In High Wycombe one can still see the ruins of the Hospital of St John, in Easton Street. It was founded before 1265 for the relief of pilgrims and later, with another leper hospital of similar date dedicated to St Margaret and St Giles, open to the destitute and sick of the community. Despite the term 'leper', true leprosy may not have been particularly common and the diagnosis embraced several skin diseases.[2]

Apart from the Black Death of 1348 little detail is known of illness in Britain until the 17th century, though Henry VIII had founded the Royal College of Physicians in 1518 and a Chartered Barber-Surgeons Company in 1540, setting in train the evolution of modern medicine. One early mention of illness locally is the grant in 1636 of a licence to Simon Mayne of Dinton and his wife, 'to eat flesh on fish days by reason of a notorious sickness'. Records from Risborough tend to tell of much sadder events, being mostly gleaned from the parish burial registers.[3] Between 14 April and 9 June 1630, for instance, the Upper Hamlet was beset by plague and '12 and supposed two more' victims were buried. The town seems to have escaped the devastating outbreak in 1665 which, though fortunately the last such to occur in Britain, has rather obscured the fact that the disease was widespread throughout most of the century.

Nature rather than medicine seemed to free the country of the plague, but replaced it with smallpox and in 1711 the register tells that 'in this year ... the Smal-pox miserably raged in the town. The Violence thereof took away many of the inhabitants and so impoverished the families that they could hardly recover themselves in several years afterwards'. There were 20 burials of victims in October alone and over a period of four weeks Sarah Cock saw Esther Cock (perhaps her mother-in-law), two daughters, a son and her husband succumb before following them herself three weeks later. Such was the fear of infection that victims were often buried at night. Smallpox was so prevalent throughout the century that, although governors of the workhouse were expected to pay for all medical attention to the inmates, the parish undertook to cover the first twenty or so cases of smallpox.

In 1798 a ray of hope was offered by the work of Edward Jenner who showed that vaccination with the mild illness cowpox gave immunity from smallpox. Despite its obvious efficacy it still met opposition a century later, provoking a letter to the *Bucks Herald* on 19 March 1881 to the effect that 'People who object to vaccination cannot be well-informed. 100 years ago every third person was marked with smallpox'. Even that writer might have found it hard to believe that, as a result of Jenner's work, the World Health Organisation would declare the world free of the disease in 1979.

73   Saunderton hostel, originally a convalescent home for children from Great Ormond Street Hospital.

Although in 1833 the Vestry voted by ten to two 'that the people with Small Pox be removed out of the town to the parish houses in Longwick'.[4] there does not seem to have been a formal 'pesthouse' in all those years of pestilence. This was probably to the patients' advantage since elsewhere such accommodation often resembled the worst refugee camp, far removed from the modern example, Saunderton Infirmary or sanatorium. This was designated the county smallpox hospital though no case was ever admitted. Originally a convalescent home attached to the Hospital for Sick Children, Great Ormond Street, it is best known for the work of the doctor and author A.J. Cronin, amongst others, in the treatment of tuberculosis. Today it provides emergency accommodation, administered by the district Social Services department.

Risborough seems to have escaped the 19th-century scourge of cholera, though it seems safe to assume that the 'Pulvemacher Galvanic Chain Belt', a popular preventive of the day and predecessor of the copper bracelet, played no part in that good fortune. A more likely reason was the abundance of springs supplying uncontaminated water and the improvement in sewage disposal since that day in 1689 when the Manor Court ordered 'all Dunghills in the Street of Princes Risborough to be removed

before the five and twentieth of the Instant Aprill upon penalty that every man that hath a Dunghill there unremoved at the tyme appointed shall forfeit twelve pence the Load, halfe to bee paid to the Lord and halfe to the poore of this parish.'[5]

In the early 19th century medical education was still hampered by prejudice, nowhere more so than in the study of anatomy. This led to the macabre crime of 'body snatching' or resurrection as its perpetrators preferred to call it. At Aylesbury Quarter Sessions in 1832 two men were sentenced to hard labour for this offence even though the Royal College of Surgeons was pointing out the absurdity of being required by charter to know anatomy but banned by common law from dissection.

Accidents made a great impact on the community, exemplified by two tragedies, 500 years apart. On 28 July 1364, two-year-old Henry Carpenter of 'Losley' fell into a vessel of boiling water 'and thus came to his death'[6] and on 19 November 1861, at the brewery, Thomas Silsby, neglecting to close a trapdoor behind him, fell into the scalding liquor in the vat below. He was rescued by Thomas Parsons, Jnr. but succumbed after lingering until the next day.

74   *(facing page)*   A more popular remedy than even the Pulvemacher Galvanic Belt.

75   Horace Ridley's pharmacy in the Market Square, c.1900.

Childbirth and infectious disease were great dangers and well into the 20th century whooping cough, diphtheria and scarlet fever closed the schools and decimated classes. Many families suffered repeated tragedy. William Wootton of Longwick buried three sons and one daughter on 29 August 1830 and the Gunnings, who had moved from London to Monks Risborough, were another example out of many:

Henry
b. January 1832
buried 21 October 1832 aged 9 months
Maria
b. August 1833
buried 5 June 1834 aged 10 months
Susan
b. December 1834
buried 14 June 1836 aged 17 months
Maria
b. c.1805
buried 18 November 1836 aged 29 years

In 1833 The Buckinghamshire General Infirmary, forerunner of our modern hospitals, opened in Aylesbury. At that time Risborough had at least four resident doctors and the Vestry arranged the first 'health service' contracts. In 1810 John Watson agreed to attend the poor of the parish for one year[7] 'in all General Illness, caught Smallpox and inoculation, accidents, Broken Bones, Amputations and all other cases whatsoever (except Midwifery)' for £25. Midwifery was charged at 10s. 6d. for each poor woman attended in the town and a guinea for those in the upper and lower hamlets.

In 1813 John Lovegrove Norris, by all accounts a much-loved man whose memorial is the larger church bell, contracted for £50, saying that, if that sum was above the Vestry's expectations, 'I have only to observe that during the time Mr. Watson attended the parish I have without any additional trouble … received from sixty to seventy pounds of the individual poor each year'.[8]

The rising cost of health care and apportionment of blame was just as hotly debated by administration and profession then as it is now. In 1835 a Poor Law Commissioner was suggesting that one doctor would suffice for the Aylesbury Union, which had responsibility for 40 parishes and a population pool of over 22,000! Not surprisingly he found that 'the medical men of Buckinghamshire had given him so

76 Lovegrove Norris's application for the post of physician to the poor.

much trouble that he would urge the guardians to procure medical officers from London'.

Throughout the 19th century the art of medicine was being refined by science, old beliefs were being questioned and many discarded. In the 20th century the process of change continues apace, to the point where now the science of medicine might benefit from the refinement of art.

Chapter Nine

Highways and Byways

ANY EXPLORATION of highways and byways around Princes Risborough must start on the Icknield Way, though so much about it is speculative that it will be historically more rewarding to examine younger roads than linger on the Way.

There is a romance to the Icknield Way, nowhere better expressed than in the account by Edward Thomas, first published in 1916.[1] He reveals his poet's soul in the opening sentence, 'Much has been written of travel, far less of the road' but later, in a prosaic moment, says it 'is sufficiently explained as the chief surviving road connecting East Anglia and the whole eastern half of the regions north of the Thames, with the west and the western half of the south of England'.

In this part of its course the Icknield Way divides into two tracks, Upper and Lower, the former and almost certainly more ancient following the lower slopes of the Chilterns and the latter crossing the open vale. The clear division into two may, in fact, only express the crystallisation with time of what was essentially a very broad path. It is interesting that the early importance of an east-west route, for so long supplanted in favour of the metropolitan south-north axis, is once again being recognised.

As it passes Princes Risborough the lower way is now almost entirely metalled and its line suggests some Roman involvement, even if superimposed on an older track. The upper way remains largely a green lane passing between banks and hedges, free of the hustle of modern traffic though threatened by political correctness in the appellation 'byway open to all traffic'. Even so, despite its immutable appearance, the Upper Icknield Way may not always

have passed so close to Risborough. The marked dog-leg diversion along the present A4010 past Culverton, taken with other land features, has led to the suggestion that west from Whiteleaf it originally kept closer to the hills, passing the present day Brimmer's Farm and Wardrobes to regain its line by crossing the A4010 at Culverton Pitches.[2]

Most early references to Buckinghamshire roads concern maintenance, or rather the lack of it. One telling comment is that of St J. Priest. who wrote in 1813

> The roads of this county are extremely bad, having ruts so deep, that when the wheels of a chaise fall into them, it is with the greatest danger that an attempt can be made to draw them out; nay, instances may be produced where, if such an attempt is made, the horse and chaise must inevitably fall into bogs. In riding from Risborough to Bledlow, my horse fell into a bog up to his chest.[3]

What a relief it must have been when, in 1815, John Loudon McAdam undertook the improvement of public roads and had the satisfaction of seeing his system of 'macadamising' commonly adopted. Based on the assumption that well-drained earth would support any load his simple device was to lay a surface of broken stone, in this area gravel, flints and 'rag', hard chalk dug from the many 'ragpits', directly on a foundation of earth raised to ensure proper drainage.

Road finance was, as always, a problem and in 1706 Turnpike Trusts were first set up, raising loans to maintain the roads and setting tolls to fund repayment. To have a more assured income tollgates were sometimes leased by auction for as long as three years at a time. The Wycombe-Aylesbury turnpike

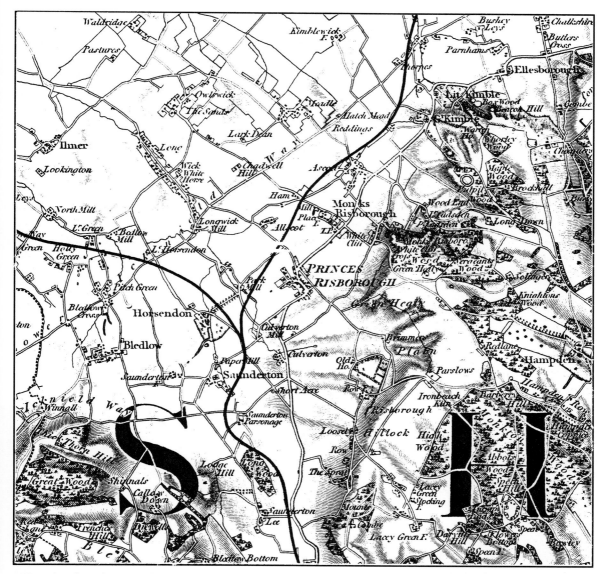

77 Taken from the 1822 Ordnance Survey. The new turnpike road from High Wycombe to Aylesbury is shown, with a gate marked TP at Monks Risborough. The GWR line from Maidenhead to Aylesbury and Oxford, which reached Risborough in 1862, has been drawn in.

led through Risborough to Terrick and thence along the present B4009 to join the A413 Wendover-Aylesbury road at Worlds End. Gates were erected at West Wycombe, Monks Risborough (by the still-standing ninth milestone), at the Lower Icknield Way junction in Little Kimble (and later at Little Kimble Church) and at Terrick from where a more convenient line to the A413 and Aylesbury was built via Stoke Mandeville in 1822-7.[4]

The section from West Wycombe to Risborough, on the line of the present A4010, was set up in 1795. A route connecting the River Thames via Wycombe and the Risborough Gap to the Icknield Way and further north had been important since earliest times but the ground traversed by the present road as far as Saunderton was marshy with at times a definite stream comparable with the Misbourne flowing through it. The track through

78   The Upper Icknield Way.

79   The West Wycombe end of the Risborough Turnpike, *c*.1907. The Pedestal marks completion of the road out of Wycombe with chalk from the caves created by Sir Francis Dashwood in 1752. Although the caves are associated with the later Hell-Fire Club Sir Francis declared 'My sole reason for making the road is the welfare of the villagers ... that they shall have employment'.

the higher and more westerly valley, which includes Deanfield and continues between Bledlow Ridge and Lodge Hill, provided a drier and better route which in its northern part is associated with a high concentration of prehistoric sites.[5]

The final stage was the road from Risborough to Thame via Longwick.[6] This provides an interesting look at local politics in action. Although

Abingdon, who owned the requisite land in Thame, wanted to acquire four miles of the existing road between Saunderton Lee and West Wycombe, the goal was in sight.

At this stage a new scheme was put forward to link Wheatley Bridge to West Wycombe via Thame and Bledlow. Lord Abingdon withdrew his support from the original proposal, making the

80   The junction at Terrick, *c.*1917, looking towards Aylesbury from the Butlers Cross road.

the first plan had been drawn up in 1794 and the necessary Act obtained in 1795, construction was delayed because of difficulties which, it was envisaged, would be remedied by the impending enclosure of Princes Risborough and Thame. The former was completed by 1824 and a good road was made northwards to the parish boundary with Aston Sandford whose road to Kingsey was also made good. As less than three miles remained between Kingsey, Towersey and Thame, and Lord

somewhat tenuous objection that an old enclosure and cottage garden of his would be interfered with and the more insulting one that the original proposal was merely a link between Thame and Risborough, a slur which led the Risborough trustees to declare a 'war of extermination'. Commonsense prevailed and the road was completed in 1825. There were two gates in Longwick, one on the main road and the other in Bar Lane, with a third added later at Kingsey.

81   Looking east to Monks Risborough from the approximate position of the former turnpike, *c.*1925.

An indication of some of the problems facing travellers before these improvements can still be seen on the right of the A4129 Risborough-Thame road at Alscot, where a deep valley is identified on an early 19th-century estate map as a 'slipe, formerly a road' in the possession of Mr. James Stratton.[7] It dropped to a ford through the stream before a bridge was built (together with one at Culverton Mill) in 1821 by one William Charge, at the expense of the enclosure Commissioners. A bridge had also been built in 1818 beside Summerleys Ford by William Lacey, at the expense of the parish.

Local roads improved considerably with enclosure of the parish though some rights of way were lost. Strong emotions were aroused then, as now, as the following letter to the Commissioners shows:

> We, the undersigned inhabitants of Loosley Row have beheld with surprise all the paths leading to the back part of the [Risborough] Baptist Meeting House and the sepulchre of our Fathers stopt up. We ... entreat you will interpose and continue the path leading from Purtwell Springs across by Barber's Pits to the Icknield Way, down the Bell Holloway to the Meeting House, and also from Burying Field along the Hays End to the Meeting House which route has been used by us and our forefathers from time immemorial for conveying corpses to the place of interment and attending a place of Public Worship.

82 The old road as it reached Monks Risborough from Askett. Walter Arnott's cottage, on the left, was demolished in the 1920s.

83 The 'slipe' at Alscot, with the modern road running above it on the left.

84 *(left)*   'Risboro' path to Whiteleaf', *c.*1930.

85 *(above)*   Barrow Way, now lost in the gardens of Windmill Hill cul-de-sac. (J. Parminter)

86 *(below)*   Poppy Road, *c.*1930. Formerly called Poppy Row, it was the old turnpike route out of town.

87 *(right)*   Looking north from Back Lane in the 1930s. Scene of the most recent highway changes, culminating in 1996 with demolition of the *Buckingham Arms*, giving way to Tesco. What was a farmhouse in the 19th century is now Wellington House Surgery and Back Lane itself is virtually a dual carriage-way.

A subsequent letter complains: 'We feel ourselves aggrieved that you did not attend to our claim'.

A benefit we still enjoy was the diversion of the turnpike at Parkfield in 1820. Prior to that one old road led to 'Culverton Water' and another descended what is now Poppy Road, both leading into the present Station Road. The Turnpike Trustees suggested an alteration to commence at 'a point opposite the corner of New Close in Parkfield in a sweep within 30 yards of the corner of the Barrow Way and come down into the existing road at or near to the Dog Kennel Park Gate' adding a few days later that 'The Trustees conceive it to be of so much importance to the Publick ... to avoid the Angle and Descent in the existing road. Some Trustees favour a line across the hill, others along the corner of the Barroway'.[8]

The 'corner of the Barrow Way' is the apex of the group of houses called Princes' Place and the curve of the Wycombe Road can easily be related to it today. The Way itself has all but disappeared, leaving a trace on the town side at the top of a few gardens but towards Culverton lost under the recently built houses of Windmill Hill.

The next major undertaking was in 1831 when 38 men were employed in levelling the hills at Culverton. At a Vestry meeting, begun in the workhouse but adjourned to the more congenial surroundings of the *George*, it was resolved 'That the First Hill at Culverton be removed from the lowest Peg to the lowest part between the two hills' and, never spendthrift,

> that an application be made to the Trustees to reimburse the Parish for the expence thereof ... that Wm Polley's offer of executing the work for 75 Pounds be accepted. Thirty seven pounds ten shillings to be paid when finished—the remaining thirty seven pounds ten shillings to be paid in twelve months.

So things remained until 1925 when extensive modernisation of the road between Aylesbury and High Wycombe was begun. At Monks Risborough it was straightened (where then was the Lord Abingdon to save Walter Arnott's cottage and garden?) and more levelling was done at Culverton Pitches. Most recent has been the widening of Back Lane in 1984 to take traffic away from the High Street while arguments still rage as fiercely as they did in 1820 about the line of a possible bypass.

Chapter Ten

The Coming of the Railway

DESPITE ITS IDEAL geographical location astride one of only four gaps in the Chiltern escarpment between the Thames and Bedfordshire, Princes Risborough was a late starter in railway development, bypassed by both the London & Birmingham Railway, which chose the Tring Gap to escape from the London Basin, and the Great Western Railway (GWR), which followed the Thames through the Goring Gap.

In the 1840s Brunel was invited by the infant Wycombe Railway Company to survey a proposed route northwards from the GWR at Maidenhead. It was this railway which eventually reached Princes Risborough in 1862 on its way to Oxford and Aylesbury and a junction was created just outside the town to serve these separate destinations. It was a single-track line, built to Brunel's broad gauge, with occasional sidings to serve local industry and

88 *(left)*   This is the earliest known photograph of Risborough station, taken by Henry Taunt soon after the line opened. The timber-faced *Railway Tavern* is behind the station, on the left.

89 *(above)*   The Saunderton cutting and tunnel.

90 *(below)*   Two early outside-frame goods engines.

farms and was operated from the outset by the GWR which took it over completely in 1867. The original station building stood a few hundred yards north of the present one, with the *Railway Tavern* facing it on the corner of Station Approach.

The Aylesbury branch became the first passenger railway to be converted from the ill-fated broad gauge to standard gauge, in 1868. This was undertaken in order to simplify operations at Aylesbury station where the line now joined the Duke of Buckingham's railway which had been built to what was later the standard gauge. The conversion of the remainder of the Wycombe line was completed in the amazing timespan of 10 days in August 1870.[1,2]

The final main line to reach London, the Great Western and Great Central Joint Railway (GW&GCR) project of the 1890s, swept away much of the Wycombe Railway route although the original Brunel trackbed can still be traced in fields south of Saunderton tunnel and a station building survives at Bledlow. Early cast-iron 'bridge' rails can also be found serving as boundary fence-posts along the present-day railway.

In the 1920s and '30s, when rail-borne freight was at its peak, a team of more than twenty personnel was employed at Princes Risborough station to

91 *(above)*　　The station in its heyday, *c.*1905.

92 *(right)*　　The footbridge and four main lines.

93 *(below)*　　The once familiar coal horse and cart collect from Timothy East's own wagons at Aylesbury station in the early 1930s.

94 The *Railway Tavern*, Witcher's garage, Station-master's house and the complexity of the junction are all shown in this 1940s aerial view.

handle both passenger and goods services. A yard on the south end of the current station, now a car park, handled local freight, and a siding served the Forest Products Research Laboratory.

Slip coaches, a GWR time-saving invention, provided regular excitement until the early 1960s when the practice was abandoned. A coach would be 'slipped' from an express train as it sped northwards down the gradient from Saunderton, coming to rest under its own braking short of the station. An engine was then dispatched to haul it the final few yards into the down platform!

As has been mentioned elsewhere, the railway led to considerable expansion of the town in the latter part of the 19th century, especially in Parkfield, partly because of the needs of its own employees but also because the junction was a considerable distance from the main conurbation, encouraging development nearer the station. Also, by facilitating the movement of goods and making coal more easily available (to be distributed by the firm of Timothy

East, based at Church End) it helped to improve living standards.

Unfortunately, little is known about the 'navvy' families who built the GW&GCR though there must have been a good number of them. It has been suggested that many were encamped near the station in the fields which are now Manor Park Avenue. They seem to have fitted well into the community and were supported by the Church of England Navvy Mission Society. The children attended the British School and a Mission Room and Sunday School were provided in 1903, thought to have been in the vicinity of Station Approach.

A hundred years after it opened, and after achieving great importance in the early 1900s, the railway was in decline and its second platform and passenger bridge became superfluous. However, all is not lost and, while feelings may run high at the thought of the possible impact of high speed freight trains on rural tranquillity, the railway, so significant in the evolution of the town, seems scheduled for survival.

Chapter Eleven

The Lion and the Bees

WHILST LIFE in Princes Risborough was never all beer and skittles, its brewery was an important feature in the 19th century and its hostelries were the focus of much more than just revelry, through Friendly Societies, slate clubs, sports teams and the like, a tradition still evident today even though their number is reduced.

Of the six inns and public houses, *Bell*, *Cross Keys*, *George and Dragon*, *Wheatsheaf*, *White Hart* and *White Lion*, listed in 1830[1] only the *White Hart*, at the south-east end of the High Street and once called the *Catherine Wheel*, has totally disappeared, replaced by modern shops. The *Bell* and *George and Dragon* still thrive, though it is uncertain whether the latter is the *George* mentioned in a previous chapter as being ancient in 1678. The remaining three are no longer licensed premises. The *Cross Keys*, once a staging post for the Thame-London coach, had become Dr. Wills' surgery by the late 1920s. The *Wheatsheaf* (which in 1820 was called the *Red Lion*) became the Capital and Counties (now Lloyds) Bank and the *White Lion* withstood a threat of demolition during the 1980s road improvements and is now offices.

95   A coaching scene from the late 19th century. (Ronald Goodearl)

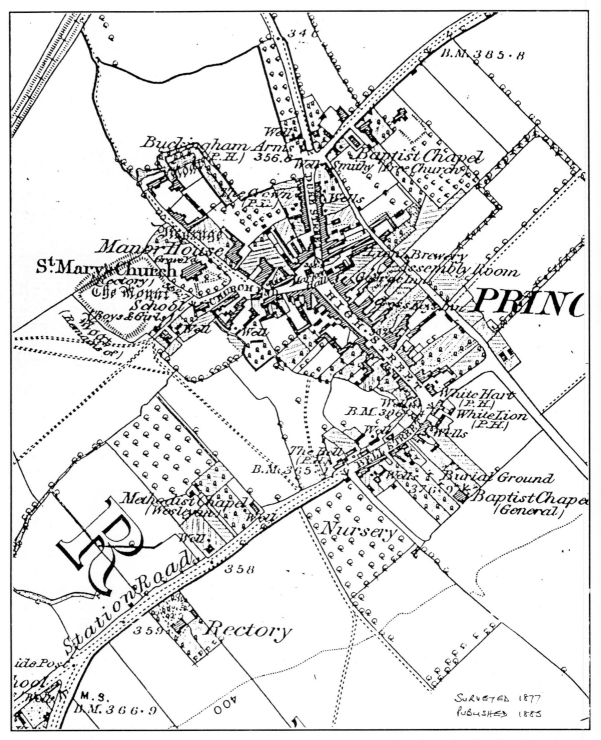

96 A larger scale view of the town centre, showing the brewery complex and main hostelries. Taken from the 1885 Ordnance Survey.

97 The *White Hart*, demolished in the 1960s.

There were several more alehouses, though most only opened on special occasions such as market days and were a subsidiary part of their landlords' livelihoods. From Aylesbury one came first to the *Buckingham Arms*, followed by the *Crown*, in Duke Street. Leonard Bull mentions an *Angel* in the vicinity of the market square but no evidence has been found to support this.[2] The *Star* in Church Street is now offices, and the *Rising Sun* at Church End is a private house.

The *Omer Pasha* has gone completely from the High Street, replaced by modern shops at 7a and 7b in the 1980s. It is said to have had an older name, *Saracen's Head*, but that its owner, William Walker of Longwick, hoping to benefit from development in Parkfield with the advent of the railway, opened a new alehouse in Station Road and gave that the established name. This was around the time of the Crimean War, 1854-6, and Thomas Barnard, who

took over the High Street premises, had a good alternative in the name of Omer Pasha, a mercenary adventurer who had captured the popular imagination.

Neither the *Saracen's Head* nor its near neighbour the *Bird in Hand* with its tiny shop, merited entries by name in local directories, the proprietors being simply identified as beer retailers. The *Railway Tavern* served an obvious need while from High Wycombe the traveller was met by the *Black Prince*, the original of which stood in what is the car park of the present 1930s hotel.

In 1830 there were two maltsters in the Market Square, Abraham Lowe and Jonathan Clarke. The latter lived at The Gables and was also a corn chandler. His business was taken over by Abel Rogers, a prominent citizen and churchwarden, who sold the house and associated family brewery in 1869, a few years before his death. What

98   Duke Street, *c.*1890, and once called Crown Lane after the beerhouse at mid-left. The *Buckingham Arms*, replaced by a 1920s version which has itself just been demolished (1996), faces up the street.

99   A reconstruction of a badly-damaged 1857 glass plate photograph of the *Omer Pasha*, whose sign should hang over the door but was the point of impact when the plate was cracked. It shows Thomas Barnard and his wife, Ann, on the day their son, Edward, was christened.

100 The former *Black Prince* was replaced, like the *Buckingham Arms* at the other end of town, to accommodate the wave of visitors to such institutions as the Forest Products Research Laboratory.

happened to the brewery equipment is not known, subsequent occupants being harness makers. A factor in the sale may have been the success of a new rival, the Lion steam brewery.

At that time two landmarks projected above the trees of Princes Risborough, its 'modest spire and too assertive brewery chimney'.[3] The Lion brewery dominated the town literally and figuratively and so too did its founder, Thomas Rogers Parsons. He came to Risborough in about 1840, living at Whiteleaf House and, on his death in November 1878, the *Bucks Herald* said of him: '... a most public spirited man ... ever ready to receive the needy or to support charitable and religious institutes. The free church was mainly promoted by him ... the same may be said of the British School.' His son Thomas followed closely in his father's footsteps, giving freely of his time and fortune to his employees and the town.

The brewery was a substantial property employing some 20-30 men directly and adding to the livelihoods of many others. Among these was the blacksmith whose forge stood in Back Lane opposite the present-day Roman Catholic presbytery. Local farmers supplied most of the barley and the Woosters of Chestnut and Rectory Farm in Monks Risborough had a contract to remove the spent hops and manure. Two huge farm carts, each one drawn by two horses, with a third to get them up the incline to Monks Risborough, made the collection every 10 days all year round.

Three separate sites were involved. The first extended from the Aylesbury road to the dray yard in Back Lane. Part of it, donated for the purpose by Thomas Parsons, was occupied by the Free Baptist church and next to it was a pair of thatched cottages occupied by the Janes and Goodchild families whose menfolk were employed at the brewery. These cottages were demolished in 1937 when St Teresa's Church was built. A meadow for the horses extended from there to the dray yard which included stables, the cooper's workshop and extensive cellars through which a stream ran in a brick channel with stone arches at entrance and exit.

Legend tells of an underground tunnel connecting the cellars with the malthouse in Church End. In 1923 the dray yard was bought by George Lacey, a local builder with a shop in Duke Street, who built a house in the meadow. His successor Jack Kibble, who was also an undertaker, made coffins in the cellars and had a chapel of rest in the old stables. The staddle stones which supported the buildings gave the modern houses, built on the site in the 1980s, their name.

Between Back Lane and the Market Square were the offices, wine and spirit stores and brewhouse with its tall chimney, demolished brick by brick in about 1927. A gated archway surmounted by a hollow statue of a lion, some eight feet long by four feet high, led into the Market Square. A swarm of bees was reputed to live in the lion and it is a matter of some regret that they were not there to protect it when, having seen so much history pass by, it was summarily destroyed in the early 1960s when the site was cleared for business development. By a curious coincidence, nearby Duke Street had been called Honey Lane long before the brewery arrived.

The third and fundamental site was the malthouse in Church End, where the barley was delivered, soaked and dried. The main building was large enough to accommodate the 400 people who feasted there to celebrate the coronation of King George V in 1910, but was overshadowed by the huge kiln which consumed five cwt. of coal a night. It was some 30ft. in diameter at its base rising about 80ft. to the tip of its weathervane. The malthouse was normally a hive of activity with men stripped to the waist handling the soaking barley.

In its heyday the Lion steam brewery produced a range of nine ales as well as stout and porter and sold a 36-gallon barrel of strong ale for 56s. Unfortunately all good things come to an end. In 1899 the London-based Welch Ale brewery bought the Lion at auction and production of Risborough beers stopped in about 1901. In 1920 Welch were

101 Charles Phillips, of Green Hailey farm, leaves the 'modest spire and too assertive brewery chimney' behind him, c.1910.

102 *(above left)*   The Lion Brewery arch and chimney, and the Market House, *c.*1910.

103 *(below left)*   The malthouse kiln, demolished *c.*1925.

bought in their turn by Watney's who off-loaded the Risborough premises to the Aylesbury Brewery Company with the proviso that they were not to be used as a brewery, nor for the sale of excisable liquors.

The malthouse was bought by Henry Laidler whose stationery company, Cheverton and Laidler, provided much needed employment in the difficult years between the wars and still thrives in the Longwick Road. The kiln was demolished quite soon but the main building survived until 1984, ending its days as the Nesta furniture factory and now replaced by the Malthouse Square complex.

Laidler was also instrumental in bringing another good employer to the town in the early years of the Second World War. This was the firm of Aston and Full, who escaped from the blitz to the British school at his suggestion.[4] After the Second World War they took over the disused wartime emergency meteorological station in Mill Lane, Monks Risborough, whose staff accommodation became Courtmoor, unpopular District Council emergency housing, now replaced by good quality homes.

The brewery was an important factor in the return of prosperity to the town in the 19th century and it is perhaps surprising that Thomas Parsons' name is nowhere publicly remembered save in the inscription on the vault in the Baptist church graveyard where he and his family lie buried. He was a considerable benefactor and a man of vision, on whose death the town closed down as a mark of respect—a veritable busy bee.

Chapter Twelve

All Work and No Play

THOUGH SCHOOLDAYS may not have been the happiest days of the children's lives in 19th-century Princes Risborough, their teachers do seem to have taken the old adage to heart and striven to avoid making Jack a dull boy. Prior to that era little is known of school life but two 18th-century charities show that education was valued.

In 1713 Katherine Pye settled land at Quash Farm, Towersey 'for educational and eleemosynary [almsgiving] purposes' in Bradenham, Hughenden, Princes Risborough, Towersey and West Wycombe with the specific aim of improving standards in English. Since 1904, when County Councils began paying teachers' salaries, the charity has been amalgamated with others of similar intent and administered centrally.

In 1772 Richard Stratton bequeathed £500 to the governors of Christ's Hospital to secure a nomination from Princes Risborough to the Bluecoat School. Those who debate the propriety of educational selection today might not have been impressed by the 'Vestry held at the Church 12th. January 1832 to elect a Boy to the Bluecoat school in the room of Thomas Grace'. It was proposed by Mr. James Stratton that 'each person vote according to his property, viz. under £50 to have one vote, £50 to have two votes and every £25 above £50 to command a vote, no person to have more than 6 votes'. William Stratton's boy, Henry, was duly elected by 80 votes to 50.

In 1881, if there had been any substantial benefit in return, the parish would have given up its rights at the Bluecoat School as conditions of entry became increasingly difficult to meet. In October 1903 the Parish Council (which had replaced the Vestry in 1894) noted that the examination standards were 'such as to preclude any candidate from the parish obtaining entrance'. As letters from the school were usually addressed to the rector they dropped the problem in his lap. Fortunately he and the boys proved them wrong and places have continued to be won.

Pigot's Directory of 1823 mentions two academies, in the names of James Crook and Mary Thorpe. The 1830 edition lists three schools in the High Street, Mary Thorpe's day and boarding school, Mary Hester's day school for girls and John Stratton's for boys, while Thomas Terry had a boys' day school at Duck End (the Horns Lane and Bell Street area).

In 1836 the British School was established on the monitorial system of the British and Foreign School Society, formerly the Lancastrian Society, founded by a Quaker, Joseph Lancaster, in 1808. Under this system, which was still used in village schools 150 years later, older pupils supervised younger ones, allowing one or two teachers to cope with, in this case, up to 139 pupils, the building having been enlarged in 1847 to accommodate that number. There was a good average attendance without the need of 'canvassing, compulsion [or] tyrannical interference with parental rights'. Since the school closed in 1913 the building, which still stands at the junction of the Station and Wycombe Roads, has been variously used as a dance hall, cinema, roller-skating rink, factory and, almost full circle, a computer-age education and communication business.

In 1841 the National School, now the Parish Hall, was built on part of the former workhouse

104 The British School opened in 1836, soon after the turnpike road was diverted from Station Road to its present line through Parkfield.

site. Promoted by the 'National Society for the Education of the Poor in the Principles of the Established Church' it was later known as the Church of England School. Although the British School was officially non-denominational and favoured by non-conformist families, both schools were open to all. They provided a good general education founded on Christian principles, though until the latter part of the century learning was very much by rote.[1]

Sectarianism raised its head only briefly; in 1881, when the National School was losing £20 a year and voluntary subscriptions were being sought to avoid a rate and the imposition of a school board. One respondent pointed out that 40 per cent of the pupils were from dissenting families and 'while intending no matter of Church and dissent' asked if they should not contribute. Rising costs meant that such 'penny schools' had to impose higher fees and in 1891, at the British School, children of farmers and shopkeepers paid 6d. (infants 4d.), those of journeymen, mechanics and foremen 4d. (infants 2d.) and of labourers 2d. all round.

School attendance was influenced by the weather, health and harvest. The latter commanded a week's holiday, determined by the season and promptly started, less promptly finished. Illness was a constant threat. In October 1887 scarlet fever kept 27 pupils away, some with it and others with a very real fear of it. In 1891 an epidemic of measles lasted for four months and in 1893-4 several children died from diphtheria.

Usually great care was taken not to jeopardise the children's health by exposure to bad weather although on one occasion a group of children from Loosley Row, arriving soaked to the skin by rain, were promptly sent the mile or so home to get dry. The headmaster of the National School once complained that some pupils used rain as an excuse for neglected homework by claiming it washed their slates clean!

Attendance was also adversely affected by social functions, though perhaps more at the National School winter evening continuation classes than at the day schools. The continuation classes were to further the education of teenagers who were already working and it is not surprising that they preferred such counter-attractions as the new Picture Palace lantern theatre which opened in November 1911. However, as the general curriculum included its own lantern lectures and outings (for example 74 children were taken by train to the Indian and Colonial Exhibition in 1886) and half-holidays were also given for local events such as the Agricultural Show with its magnificent fruit and vegetable display in the High Street, so the teachers could justifiably complain. Even Samuel Dyer, whose term of office as headmaster of the National School from 1904-19 was a Golden Age, was moved to comment sourly of the October 'Bang-all' fair in 1918 that it 'consisted of three caravans and a booth attached to each. The temptation to spend the evening in mud with two flares and three wretched booths was too strong for all but nine boys and eight girls'.

Dyer must have been a remarkable man. Apart from improving educational standards, he introduced such things as football, cricket and boxing for the boys and hockey for the girls. In 1913 he led the school choir to first prize in the Berks, Bucks and Oxon music competition. He also formed an air rifle club which in 1915 defeated a team from 8 Company, Royal Engineers, though it was graciously acknowledged that 'the guns and ammunition were entirely different from what the engineers were used to'.

Discipline was generally good and teachers today would welcome the uncomplicated report of an inspector who, in 1885, was 'very pleased with the good conduct and attention of the Dear Children'. Perhaps writing and personally handing over their own reports to their parents had some bearing. Louisa, daughter of local farmer and photographer Leonard Pauling who later emigrated with his family

105 Samuel Dyer with his pupils at the National School. Fred Jacobs, from the High Street garage, is fourth from the right in the middle row.

106 'Our motto is – be brave' reads the board to Mr. Dyer's left. The National School infants in 1906, among them the young Ernie Goodchild, on their best behaviour.

to New Zealand, was a good pupil but there were exceptions. On an unlucky 13 June 1887 at the British School, 'Albert Kingham, being insolent, was punished with the rod. He threatened to strike the master [Samuel Jordan] and refusing to apologise, was dismissed. He returned on 14 June and apologised'. At the National School it had been resolved in 1871 that corporal punishment would be abandoned, so Charles Jacobs was simply expelled in 1899 for his crime of 'persistently making the others laugh'. The resolution was subsequently rescinded. In the same year the master, James Royston, attributed poor attendance at the evening class to 'the firm attitude I found it necessary to adopt … when some of the boys attempted to take liberties. One was trying to light a cigarette and I immediately spoke out on the matter'.

In 1861 George Eggleton established his Chiltern college in Queen's Road 'for the purpose of meeting the great demand for a sound middle-class education in this district'.[2] It had a typical grammar school curriculum and immediately attracted over forty pupils. Its success was short-lived for, although it appears on the 1877 Ordnance Survey as the only building in the road, the same site has a new name, Chiltern Cottage, by 1889 and this refers to the 'six newly erected cottages' which still stand, built on the site and sold by James Stephens of Oxford to Susan West of 14 Connaught Place, Hyde Park.

Little is known of early adult education but from the mid-19th century evening lectures on practical matters such as improving allotments were offered by 'technical officers'. So important was this basic skill that allotments were provided at the British School in 1910 so that the children could also learn the rudiments of gardening.

The British School closed in 1913 and its pupils were transferred to the new Council or Bell Street

107 In 1913 the National School choir took 1st prize in the Berks, Bucks & Oxon music competition.

108 Louisa Pauling's school report, 17 July 1896. Good attendance was paramount.

Monks Risboro. N. S.
17. 7. 96

My Dear Parents.
      The first quarter of
the school year is now ended. I have
been here 94 times out of 109. Master sends
his kind regards and hopes you will keep
me regular till the holidays
            Your loving Louisa

109 *(left)*   The Bell Street Council School opened in 1913 and is now incorporated into the Gatensbury Place flats.

110 *(below)*   During the First World War the allotments at the Bell Street school served a dual purpose.

School. The National School survived (as Church End County Primary School) until 1963 when its pupils were the first intake of Berndene County Combined School in Wellington Avenue. Finally, in 1981 both groups were united at Berndene which was renamed Icknield County Middle School. The Secondary or Upper School opened in 1949 and Berryfield County First School in 1969. A girls' convent school was established by the Daughters of Jesus, first at Wellington House, later across the road beside the Walsingham Hall. When the Order left Risborough the school, St Teresa's, passed into private hands, admitting girls and boys. It is the only surviving independent school in the town.

In these modern times more children travel to complete their schooling than the one Bluecoat boy envisaged by Richard Stratton, but in Risborough all the schools thrive and the standard of education ensures that today neither Jack nor Jill is a dull child.

Chapter Thirteen

Sport and Recreation

IN AN AGRICULTURAL community, when the farm worker laboured from 5 a.m. to 7 p.m. in summer and from dawn to dusk in winter, there was little time for recreation except on a Sunday and even that was often strictly controlled. The earliest 'sporting news' of Risborough does, however, have the familiar ring of minor hooliganism. At the Manor Court in 1499 a penalty or 'amercement' was imposed, the amount being written in superscript, on William Bollar[2d], who 'gave illicit words to John Halys (a juror) in playing Lez Bowlys'. In 1500, simply playing the game was enough to incur a penalty—'Henry Nele[4d] and John Skytwell[4d] are common players at Lez Bowlys therefore they are amerced'.

While bear-baiting and cock-fighting were accepted as normal, the majority of pastimes seem to have been healthy for mind and body. James I listed among lawful recreation 'dancing, either men or women, archery for men, leaping, vaulting …

111 'In an agricultural community there was little time for recreation.'

112 The Maypole dance celebrating the Jubilee of King George V, 6 May 1935. (Ronald Goodearl)

113 The approach to Velvet Lawn, Little Kimble.

114   An early dramatic production at the British School, possibly *A Midsummer Night's Dream*.

Morris dances and the setting up of May-poles'.[1] Archery was certainly more acceptable than the 'amusement' prevalent in 1885 of firing at swallows with pistols! Archery practice was held at sites called 'butts' and this name is still given to the area near St Mary's Church leading to Manor Park. Early maps also show that there were Back Gate Butts, now built over, at the south-eastern end of the former Back Lane.

For the more bucolic in the 19th century there were picnics and displays at Velvet Lawn, Great Kimble, a Chiltern 'bottom' carpeted with fine grass and surrounded by natural box. In 1891, Robert Gibbs said, 'Few there are of the neighbourhood who have not spent some happy hours in that rural and lovely retreat'.[2] Sad to say, public access is now denied because of the need for security on the Chequers estate.

In the same era reports of organised enter-tainment began to appear in the local press though some were far from encouraging. In 1881 the *Bucks Herald* reported that, when Miss Lenington's Dramatic Company visited the town, 'the second

performance was so poorly attended that the management decided not to give it', adding that the fault lay with the company for returning too soon after its previous visit.

In 1911 a Picture Palace opened at the [Chalfont?] hall, giving 'magic lantern' shows. Then, in 1924, the former British School opened as the Chaplin cinema. It was taken over after three months by Mrs. Ada Wright and her sons who had left the Isle of Wight and an ailing family grocery business, persuaded by the younger son, Len, who at 13 was already an authority on the film industry. Renamed Princes, it seated 100-120 on Windsor chairs, battened together and with the end legs of each row set in a hole to keep them more or less rigid in case of panic.[3]

Films were chosen from a daily postal newsletter. 'Unreservedly recommended' or 'suitable for navvies' meant a full house but 'suitable for a sophisticated audience' had no appeal for Risborough. Silent films were accompanied by a pianist with occasional competition from a sheepdog which had learnt that bars of chocolate were

115   The Princes cinema, formerly the British School.

116   A post-war view of the Carlton cinema, opened in 1937, with the house of Mr. Stow, the manager, in the background.

117 *(above)* Princes Risborough Swimming Club in 1914. Major Coningsby Disraeli, the President, stands behind his wife. On the left of the front row is Arthur Lacey and beside him, Samuel Dyer. On the extreme right is William Chalfont.

forthcoming for the price of a few barks during the most romantic scenes.

The first 'talkie' was a fictitious version of the Titanic disaster, the last was Gracie Fields in *The Show Goes On*, a gesture of defiance before the Princes closed, unable to compete with the Carlton cinema. That opened in 1937, on the site now occupied by Carlton Court. The subsequent history of the Princes cinema has been recounted in the preceding chapter. Suffice it to say here that the future of this historically interesting building seems

secure for the moment. The Carlton was not so fortunate. It too ceased to operate as a cinema in the late 1950s and after re-opening as a bingo hall in 1961, it came to a dramatic end in 1964 when it burnt to the ground.

More healthy relaxation, if one discounts the 'smoking concerts' given to raise funds, was provided by the Swimming Club, established in 1906 by Samuel Dyer, master of the National School, and Frank Watson, a local doctor, with Major Coningsby Disraeli of Horsenden, nephew of Benjamin Disraeli, as its first president. At one time it had 99 men and boys as swimming members, and three lady subscribers! As the Parish Council was unable to provide a bathing place the club used

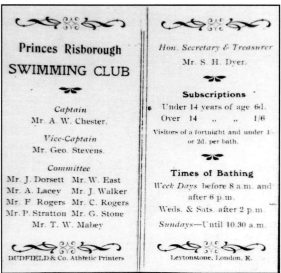

118 Arthur Lacey's membership ticket.

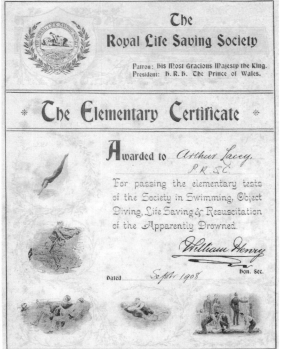

119 *(above)* Arthur Lacey's Life Saving certificate, 1908.

120 *(left)* The Club trophy, awarded anually. It was recovered in the 1960s by one of the authors, having being lost for some thirty years. The topmost shield, dated 1907, bears the name E. Evans and the succeeding seven champions were: L. Vautier, C. Rutland, F. Foster, S. Rutland, C. Humphrey, W. Crook and, again, C. Humphrey.

121 *(above)*   Herts MCC Hill climb at Kop Hill *c.*1910. The official car closing the hill is thought to be a 1908 ohc 1208cc Isotta–Fraschini, awarded the Grand Prix desVoiturettes. (A.B. Demaus)

122 *(right)*   Gripper ascends Kop Hill in a 3–litre Bentley during an Essex MC event in 1924. Today the road is enclosed by hedges and it is hard to imagine the vast number of spectators which invited disaster. (A.B.Demaus)

Longwick millpond. However, by the end of the First World War that and the only other suitable pond, at Culverton, had silted up and swimming was abandoned. Despite that, the club lived on until 1948, ever hopeful that a pool would be built, an ambition not fulfilled until 1994.

Risborough was put on the national sporting map by the Kop Hill Climb for motor cycles and cars. Kop Hill, formerly Cop or Copthill, acquired its 'K' after the Boer War. With its testing chalk surface and maximum gradient of 1 in 6 it challenged some famous names, among them Donald Campbell, Frazer Nash and Raymond Mays, not forgetting the dashing founder and headmistress of the one-time Chiltern school in Monks Risborough, Mrs. Daisy Moore, in her 'GN' Godfrey and Nash

sports car. Other equally famous machines tackling the hill included Douglas, Triumph and Zenith among the bikes, Aston-Martin, Bugatti and Hispano-Suiza among the cars (not to mention Broome & Wade's Churchill tanks during the Second World War).

A report of an Essex Motor Club event paints a graphic image:

a musical roar like the exhaust note of an aeroplane, as the eight-cylinder in-line Ballot tore up the hill … holding the road like a leech it flew up the sharpest gradient … at about 80 mph. One caught only a fleeting glimpse of Count Zborowski … G.A. Vandervell, in the 4½-litre Sunbeam, roared up … doing a terrific swerve into the bank at the summit … stones flew everywhere, while the air was filled with the reek of dust and castor oil.[4]

123   An outing to the 1924 Wembley exhibition.

The first climb took place in 1910, the last on 28 March 1925. The latter occasion was marred by two accidents, one involving T.R. Allchin on a Zenith-Blackburn 998cc. motor cycle and the second, more serious, when a Brescia-Bugatti went out of control and after two near misses eventually injured one of the many spectators who lined the edge of the road. There had been increasing anxiety at the difficulty of controlling the huge crowds which gathered, bearing in mind that stewards relied on megaphones and the ascent could be achieved in less than 30 seconds, and after these two mishaps speed racing on open roads was banned.

Returning to gentler pursuits, the town was the first to respond to an appeal made shortly before his death by King George V on behalf of the nation's

124   A more sedate East family outing of the same era, c.1910.

125   Princes Risborough Football Club 1908-9. The ubiquitous Arthur Lacey is second from the right in the front row.

126   The Whiteleaf Ladies' XI. 'Pa' Quint umpired while his three daughters played. 'Puck' third from the left, back row, Sybil third from the left, front row, with Gwen on her right and the mascot doing something very strange in front of her.

127   The young have their day. Winter sports in Poppy Road, c.1910.

children. In June 1937 the recreation ground off the Aylesbury Road was opened by Lord Derby, made possible by the generosity of Ernest Turner J.P., who gave the land opposite his house to the parish.

Nowadays it is possible to play Lez Bowlys with a clear conscience and many other sporting activities are well-supported in the town and surrounding district. It may seem strange to take as an example of this enthusiasm a team which no longer exists, but it was one which not only reflected the all-round involvement of the community but also the strong family ties which are still apparent today. The Saunderton Ladies XI was formed in about 1926, soon changing its name to the Whiteleaf Ladies XI. It was active for some ten years and at its heart were the three Quint sisters of Askett and their sister-in-law, often umpired by their father. The club provided three members of the England XI, Gwen and Puck Quint with Betty Lavington, but was equally proud of bowling out the Brill Ladies for three runs.

The town council promotes sports facilities for all ages, but the words of George V are still remembered: 'Take care of the young and the Country will take care of itself'.

Chapter Fourteen

The Home Front

IN ACKNOWLEDGING the debt owed to all those who serve the community in time of need, whether in peace or war, it seems appropriate for the fire brigade and home guard to stand as their representatives.

Fire was an ever-present threat in days of timber and thatch, not only for the immediate danger to life and property but also because it could leave a family destitute. Insurance offices, with their familiar wall plaques indicating acceptance of risk, were few and far between before the 19th century and victims were dependent on charity. Mention has already been made of a disastrous fire in 1698 which destroyed seven houses in the town. Then the Justices ordered that £30 should be distributed to the homeless families of Thomas, Francis and William Bowler, William, Thomas and John Beddall and Robert Stratton.[1]

Mills and farms were particularly at risk. In 1743 Bledlow North Mill and the house next to it were burnt down and in 1864 a fire, 'caused, it is supposed, by a tobacco pipe'[2] destroyed 16 ricks and all the buildings on John Eggleton's farm at Ilmer. In this century Culverton and Ellesborough mills suffered the same fate.

The Princes Risborough Volunteer Fire Brigade was formed in 1870, led by Captain George Stratton. No doubt the town had been influenced by a visit from members of the proposed Wycombe brigade, who demonstrated a fire engine from Merryweather & Sons in December 1868, drawing water by suction from a large well and amazing the onlookers by the throw of water.[3]

The fire engine was kept at Church End on the premises of Timothy East, who was a substantial coal merchant and fell-monger, one of a prominent

128 Princes Risborough Volunteer Fire Brigade at Church End in 1877.

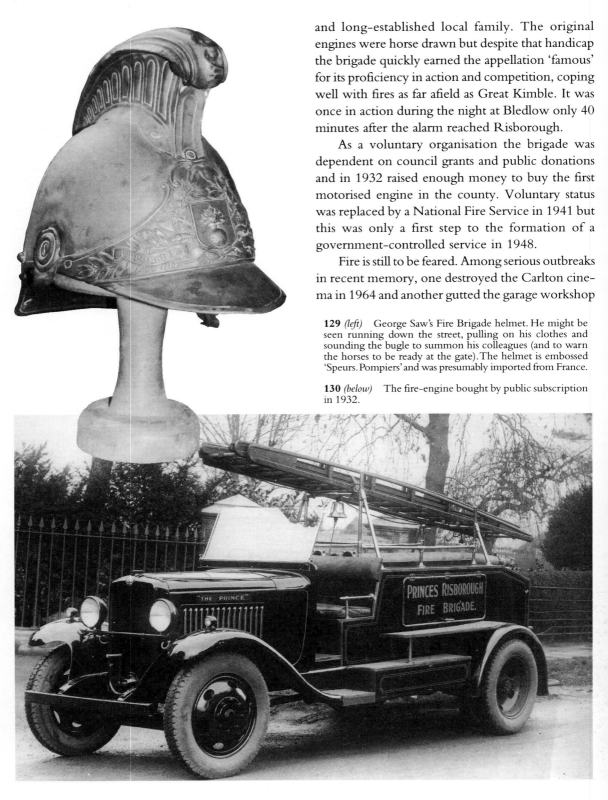

and long-established local family. The original engines were horse drawn but despite that handicap the brigade quickly earned the appellation 'famous' for its proficiency in action and competition, coping well with fires as far afield as Great Kimble. It was once in action during the night at Bledlow only 40 minutes after the alarm reached Risborough.

As a voluntary organisation the brigade was dependent on council grants and public donations and in 1932 raised enough money to buy the first motorised engine in the county. Voluntary status was replaced by a National Fire Service in 1941 but this was only a first step to the formation of a government-controlled service in 1948.

Fire is still to be feared. Among serious outbreaks in recent memory, one destroyed the Carlton cinema in 1964 and another gutted the garage workshop

129 *(left)*   George Saw's Fire Brigade helmet. He might be seen running down the street, pulling on his clothes and sounding the bugle to summon his colleagues (and to warn the horses to be ready at the gate). The helmet is embossed 'Speurs. Pompiers' and was presumably imported from France.

130 *(below)*   The fire-engine bought by public subscription in 1932.

131   First World War signal practice on land now built over between Station and Manor Roads.

132   George 'Skipper' Lacey and Ron Wood man the now-overgrown Observer Corps post above Princes Place, the corner of the old Barrow Way.

of Witcher Brothers in 1976, despite the skill, bravery and sophisticated equipment of the modern brigade.

During two world wars the home guard watched over the neighbourhood. Between 1914–18 the local corps drilled, appropriately, on the Backgate Butts, wearing their everyday clothes with as much pride as any uniformed soldier. Unfortunately they left few records and so, although outside the intended timespan of this book, the deeds of Princes Risborough 'A' Company, 1940-45, stand as a testimonial to them both.

Battle Headquarters were the Assembly Rooms behind the *George* or, should that fall into enemy hands, at the *White Lion*. The objectives were simple: 'to observe and report enemy landings' but a directive from Lt. Col. H. Beaumont, O.B.E., on 23 May 1941 suggested that

> it would be a great help if [they] were reminded … of their duty not only to arrest baled out airmen but to … instil into all citizens that they really must do something about it if an enemy airman wants to surrender. After all, if they take the trouble to come over and bale out it is not right for anyone to totally disregard them'.[4]

Banter disguised the determination of a roll-call of up to 498 volunteers, including over 70

133 *(left)* On 31 October 1920, after Major Coningsby Disraeli had unveiled the memorial tablet, the newly-restored Market House was dedicated as the First World War memorial by the Bishop of Buckingham.

134 *(above)* Princes Risborough Home guard 1941/2. William Barnard, who lent this photo, is standing fifth from the left and Frank Pavry, one of the excavators of the Black Prince's manor, is sitting second right.

135 *(right)* Also part of the First World War memorial, the District Nurse's cottage, 37 Wycombe Road, when newly-built in 1920. It is now headquarters of the St John Ambulance Division.

136   Dedication of the Red Cross and St John ambulance presented to the town in 1938 by Henry Laidler, whose premises are in the background, and William Walker of Longwick, who stands modestly at the right of the back row. Two much-loved figures are the Rev. John Gower Williams, rector from 1918-53, and on the extreme right front, District Nurse Christian Cuthbert who retired in 1956 after delivering most of the town's babies over 30 years.

137   Second World War Community Spirit.

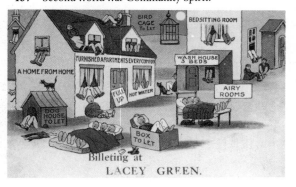

enthusiastic women. They 'manned' eight observation posts from Haddenham to Bradenham, but were not to be confused with the Observer Corps whose post was on the hill above Princes Place, still one of the best places to view the Chilterns and Vale. They trained realistically, though all mock battles would move on if ordered to do so by a policeman. They worked closely with the fire brigade which, in one exercise, pumped water copiously on a house which had the misfortune to be marked on the programme as being in flames.

138   David Hunt, of the Oxon & Bucks Light Infantry Cadet Force, Risborough Unit, guards a 'doodle-bug' or V-1 bomb which fell harmlessly on Kimblewick Farm, 1945.

139   Gathering at Church End for the VE Day parade.

That they chose to recount their story with humour and enjoyed their own-given title of 'Dad's Army' cannot obscure the fact that without the proficiency of the home guard the D-Day landings could not have been allowed to proceed for fear of leaving the country too vulnerable.

In closing this chapter mention should be made of the British Legion which was established in the town in 1927 when 126 members were enrolled at the inaugural meeting. Originally the legion met at either the Chalfont Hall or Literary Institute but in 1945 it was proposed that a hall, which could also used by the community, be built as a memorial to those who fell in the Second World War. This idea complemented the provision in 1920 of a cottage for the District Nurse, as part of the town's First World War memorial, and which is now head-quarters of the St John Ambulance division, admin-istered as a medical charity, the War Memorial Trust.

The Memorial Hall was a labour of love. The first turf was cut on 3 December 1949 and members worked voluntarily for seven years to complete the building. Although it is often invidious to single out an individual in such an organisation no-one would begrudge so small a token to the late Cyril White who became its embodiment, serving actively for more than forty years from its foundation, filling every major office at one time or another.

140 *(left)* A dinner for the recently formed British Legion branch in the Chalfont Hall, *c.*1935.

141 *(below)* Cyril White lays one of the two Foundation stones at the British Legion Hall on 5 May 1951.

Epilogue

DURING THE 19TH CENTURY there was more change than in the previous five hundred years. Education advanced, administration passed from the Vestry to a newly-created Parish Council, itself answerable to district and county bodies, and central government was playing an ever-increasing part in local affairs. Although the local economy was still based on agriculture, despite the changes brought about by enclosure, that influence had been declining since the end of the 'golden age' of farming, the 20-year period after the Crimean War when Britain was at peace and Europe was still bickering internally.

The advent of the railway paved the way for expansion but the impetus could not be sustained and the last twenty years of the century saw the beginning of a depression which was to persist until the 1930s, only briefly relieved by the demands of the First World War. By 1900, population growth was virtually at a standstill and new blood was needed to advance the 'town' which, despite all its progress, was still thought of as a village by most of its inhabitants, who still lived within the confines of the medieval boundaries. A new stimulus was needed and it came in the form of land for building.

It was, perhaps, indicative of the collapse of old ways that at Culverton, where milling had probably

142   Culverton Mill from Picts Lane.

143 *(below)* Culverton Mill.

144 *(right)* The cottage in the Mill House garden.

145 *(below left)* Plan of Culverton Estate sale.

146 *(below right)* Title page of Culverton sale brochure.

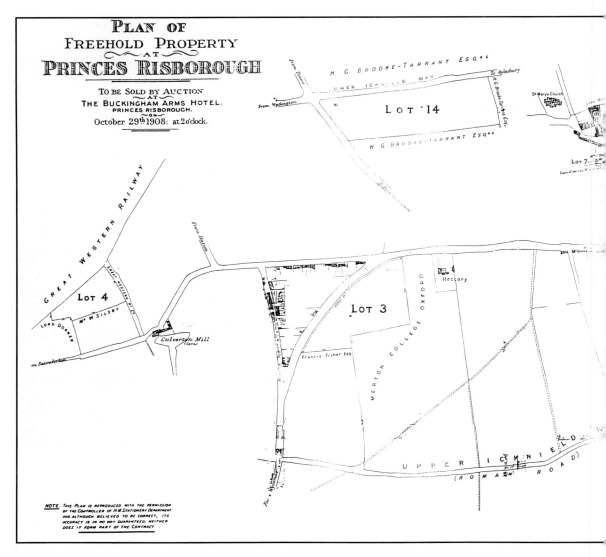

been carried on since Domesday, the 18-ft. diameter overshot wheel was losing its power because the stream below was silting up and preventing the escape of water.[1] This may have encouraged the sale of the 'Culverton Building Estate' in 1903 which led to the rapid expansion of Parkfield. A similar major sale in 1908 released more land on the south side of the Wycombe Road and, more importantly, south-east of the High Street in pre-enclosure Burying Field and Crossfield. Development in the latter areas was delayed by the two World Wars but also, fortunately, kept within reasonable bounds by the acquisition of the fields immediately below

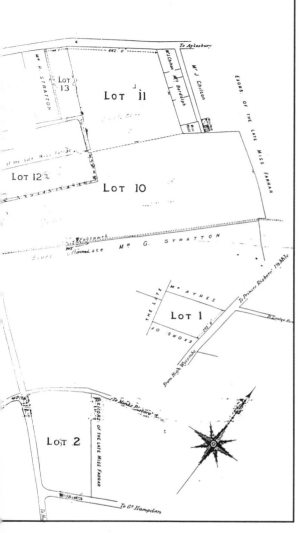

147 *(left)*   Plan of 1908 sale of land for building.

148 *(above)*   The footpath to Whiteleaf, showing the Berryfield and Woodfield land.

149 *(below left)*   Stan Wood with horse-drawn reaper-binder.

150 *(below right)*   Wood's tractor-drawn reaper-binder.

151 *(above left)*   The forge at Monks Risborough.

152 *(above)*   Tom Cummings moves with the times at Monks Risborough.

153 *(below)*   The motor car was well-catered for with the arrival of the Witcher brothers in the Station Approach in 1922.

Whiteleaf Cross by the National Trust, founded in 1895, which helped to preserve what the artist Paul Nash described in *The Times* as 'the finest view in the south of England'.

Most of the new houses in the Wycombe Road were built between the wars as were those of Cannon Place and part of Clifford Road, the latter first known as the Icknield Estate. Major development was deferred until the end of the Second World War and the compulsory purchase of fields on both sides of New Road Hill, belonging to Town Farm in Church Street. The Wood family who farmed these fields had come to Risborough in the late 19th century and can still recount at first hand in 1997 the many changes since their arrival, including the gradual replacement of the heavy horse by the tractor and the advent of the combine harvester, but which are themselves sometimes part

154 The Forest Products laboratory was established in 1925, achieving world-wide renown. It closed in 1988 when its work was transferred to Garston, and the site now accommodates small businesses. (*Bucks Herald*)

155   The Town Farm herd takes a leisurely stroll through the High Street in 1945.

of a cycle, as for instance the virtual disappearance of sheep early this century to be replaced by milk and beef cattle and their return in the wake of bovine encephalitis.

The name 'Burying Field' (an old spelling was 'Berrian' as Icknield was 'Acknell') probably referred to the bury or burgh and it became Berryfield Road. It was followed by Ash and other 'tree' roads and, in 1956, by the Woodfield complex, acknowledging the Woods' association with the land. The 1950s also saw the establishment of Molins Machine Company at Saunderton and the consequent development of Fairway for their employees, on what had previously been known as the Salt marshes, an area of springs now largely culverted.

Wellington Farm, on the north-eastern aspect of the town and probably given that name, like Duke Street, in honour of the Duke of Wellington, was built over in the 1960s and its neighbour, Place Farm in Monks Risborough, a few years later. A pretence at keeping the two developments separate by leaving a hedge across Westmead was soon abandoned, quite reasonably as the two civil parishes had been united in 1934 when the lower hamlets became 'Longwick-cum-Ilmer' and the upper hamlets 'Lacey Green'.

On the north-west Manor Park Avenue was built over the old royal park in the 1930s and in the 1960s Stratton Road (named after another long-established Risborough family) completed the encirclement of the old town.

Among significant businesses which helped to fashion the modern town the brewery, Cheverton and Laidler, and Aston and Full are mentioned elsewhere. The names of Samuel Adcock and Harold Percival, Charles Bloss and Timothy East,

156 *(above)*   Princes Risborough in 1931. The Bell Street Post Office is just being built and Cannon Place in the background has just extended the town beyond its 18th-century boundaries. (Hunting Aerofilms)

157 *(right)*   Princes Risborough in 1980. The factories of Cheverton & Laidler and Leo Laboratories, in the left background, have breached the Aylesbury branch line but the march of progress has generally been kind and the heart of the town still preserves the basic pattern of its medieval counterpart. (*Bucks Herald*)

158 This photograph from 1942 shows Albert Wainwright (far right) with his wife (far left), daughter and three sons, and employees who were as much part of the family. He built up his business from small beginnings in Dinton, travelling the district on a cycle similar to that used at this time by his son Jim (fourth from right) before moving here to Station Road. His grandsons now maintain family traditions in the High Street.

which epitomise the early 20th century, are no longer seen on shop fronts, but their family traditions are maintained by successors such as Wainwright & Sons. The furniture manufacturer, Goodearl, founded in High Wycombe in 1870, came to Risborough in 1919, initially with a small assembly room at the British School but soon moving to Picts Lane and Station Approach with eventually more than 500 employees. Another significant entrepreneur was Hubert Newitt whose business began with a cycle shop in Duke Street and progressed to agricultural engineering, pipe-laying and road-building.

The age of the motor car saw blacksmiths such as the Jacobs family in the High Street and Arthur, known as 'Tom', Cummings in Monks Risborough, learning new skills to pit against specialists such as the Witcher brothers, established in Station Approach in 1922. The Department of Scientific and Industrial Research added a new dimension to employment and outlook in the town with the establishment of the Forest Products Research Laboratory in Summerleys Road in 1925. It was an appropriate siting, arising initially out of the need to explore the use of other timbers than beech but ultimately ensuring that the name of Princes Risborough was known throughout the world by its work on every aspect of wood science. Known affectionately as The Lab, it made a significant contribution to the town for the next 50 years, bringing new philosophies not altogether lost by its transfer to Garston in Hertfordshire in 1988.[2]

Princes Risborough has completed the long journey from the Stone Age to the Age of Technology. The lost ritual of the daily stately passage of milking cows to and from Town Farm and the passing of Mr. Churchwarden Bass in 1916, 'the last farmer hereabouts to habitually wear a smock, and is to be buried in one',[3] are symbolic and Risborough present is ready to take on the future.

Appendix 1

'The Bounds of the Parish of Princess Risborough as they were taken in a survey Anno 1620'[1]

1. Begins in ye Way which leads from Princess [sic] Risborough to Monks Risborough,
2. from thence to a place called Lordless Gore [by]
3. & from thence to a Cross upon a Hill call'd Windsor Hill,
4. & from thence to a Cross upon Rudgway
5. from thence to a Cross called Chapmans Cross,
6. from thence to a place where there stood a certain Beech call'd Iron Beech,
7. from thence to an Angle or Corner of a Wood call'd Abbotts Wood,
8. from thence to a Cross behind ye House of Rich. Barrow Gent;
9. from thence to an Ash call'd Wallers Ash,
10. from thence to a Cross in Bromond Green,
11. from thence to a Cross in the field of Ralph Stone,
12. from thence to ye gate of a house of Thomas Bastion, excluding ye house aforesaid, from that gate to a Gate called Callow Hill gate,
13. from thence to a Gate in a Lane call'd little lane from ye same Gate by a Hedge to Horsingdon Mill excluding ye Mill,
14. from thence over or through a Hedge of Westie including a certain part of a Close of Ralph Cotton call'd Patten Close, by estimation three acres being an Angle or Corner of ye aforesaid Close'
15. and from ye same Angle or Corner over or through a Hedge extending over ye land of ye aforesaid Ralph Cotton to a way call'd Akman Street,
16. & over ye same way into a Close of Ralph Cotton including ye aforesaid Close except one acre
17. & so returning to a way over ye brook there into an Angle call'd Chedg Hill corner and from the same corner to a gate of a Close call'd Mill Close Gate,
18. and from the same Gate by a Highway unto ye end of the village of Ilmer,
19. & bye said Village through a Close call'd Frisses Close including the said Close unto a Cross there
20. & so by a way unto a Cross in a Corner called Sandes Corner,
21. from thence to a Gate called Barnesfield Gate,
22. from thence to a Cross called Burrow Ash Cross,
23. from thence to an Ash called Culvers Ash,
24. from thence bye bounds between the Mannor of Princess Risborough & ye said Mannor of Monks Risborough to the Place first above named.

Mr. Rex Kidd, whose documentation of records appertaining to Risborough has been invaluable, has suggested modern equivalents of the reference points mentioned, several of which are included in the following list matched to the above numbers which were inserted by the authors:

3. Windsor Hill has the same name today
5. Possibly by the Pink and Lily
6. Ironbeech Kiln was beside Lily Bank Farm on the 1885 Ordnance Survey
9. Wallers Ash = Walters Ash
12. Thomas Bastion lived at Smallden Farm
13. Little Lane was the pre-turnpike Wycombe Road via Loosley Row
14. The Forest Products laboratory, now Princes Estate, was built on Westie or West Eye
15. Akman Street = Lower Icknield Way
17. Bledlow Mill
21. Barnesfield Gate was probably in Bar Lane, Longwick
23. The Will of Thomas Loosley of Alscot, 1561, mentions 'Colverhouse Acre'

Appendix 2

Text of Copyhold admission to Number 28 Bell Street, Princes Risborough 16 May 1770

The Manor of Princes Risborough in the County of Bucks

At the View of Frank-Pledge with the **Court Baron** of John Grubb Esq. Lord of the Manor aforesaid there holden the Sixteenth Day of May In the Fourth year of the Reign of our Sovereign Lord George the Third by the Grace of God of Great Britain ffrance and Ireland King Defender of the faith &c And in the Year of our Lord One Thousand and Seven hundred and Seventy Before Thomas Plaistowe Gent. Steward of the foresaid Manor (amongst other Things) it is thus Inrolled (to wit)

Also at this Court It is Presented by the Homage That Free Brooks of Chepping Wycombe in the County of Bucks Miller a Customary Tenant of the said Manor Did out of Court (to wit) the Twenty fourth day of February last Surrender into the Hands of the Lord of the said Manor by the Rod according to the Custom of the said Manor by the Hands and acceptance of John Carruthers and John Vaughan two other Customary Tenants of the said Manor All that Customary or Copyhold Cottage or Tenement wherein George West then dwelt situate standing and being in Princes Risborough afores^d. adjoyning to a Cottage or Tenement of James Henley on the North East And also an Orchard or Close of Grass Ground to the same belonging adjoyning to the Land of John Knapp South West and to the Hayes End South East And also all Houses Outhouses Edifices Buildings Yards Gardens Orchards Backsides Hedges Ditches Trees Mounds Fences Ways Waters Watercourses Easements Comons Comon of Pasture Comoditys Hereditaments and Appurtenances whatsoever to the said appertaining **To the use and Behoof** of the said George West Occupier of the said premifses and of his Heirs and Afsigns for ever according to the Custom of the said Manor **And Now** to this Court cometh the said George West in his own proper Person and desireth of the Lord of the said Manor to be admitted Tenant to the Premises aforesaid with the Appurtenances **To Whom** the Lord by his said Steward **Granteth** Seizin thereof by the Rod **To Have and to Hold** all and Singular the said Premises with the Appurtenances unto the said George West his Heirs and Afsigns for ever Of the Lord of the said Manor by the Rod at the will of the Lord according to the Custom of the Manor aforsd. by the Yearly Rent of One Shilling Fealty Suit of Court Herriot and other Services therefore formerly due and of right accustomed He gives to the Lord for a Fine for such his Estate so to be had in the Premises as appears and so forth and the said George West is admitted Tenant thereof and doth -ffealty to the Lord for the same

Examined by me Thos. Plaistow
Stew^d of the S^d Manor.

Appendix 3

Letter of opposition to Inclosure from Rev. John Shepherd to Mr. Tindal, Solicitor to the Proponents of the scheme[1]

12th. Oct 1819

I received yr letter yesterday and confess myself rather surpriz'd at its contents supposing it was well understood that most of the inhabitants of Princes Risborough were against the propos'd Inclosure as utterly subversive of their privileges. I beg leave to inform you, Sir, whatever may be the opinion or conduct of others that I think Inclosures truly oppressive, that they have in various parts of the Kingdom (not forgetting Bledlow) cramped the hand of the industrious cottagers and brought many on the Parish. I remember what is written Proverbs 14: 31[2] & 22: 2.3[3] and therefore (for my own part, as I am forbidden to break the 8th Commandment)[4] I will draw on my head the curse of the Poor, by setting my hand to a measure so oppressive for the purpose of enriching a few Individuals

I am, Sir, Yr. most hbe Servt.   Jn. Shepherd

Notes

Chapter One
1   J. Wise, *Rec. Bucks.*, vol.33 (1991), pp.108-13.
2   Bodleian Library, Browne Willis Mss 'Crux Saxonica' ref. RAWL.40.52.opp.p.34.
3   M. Farley and S. Browne, *Rec. Bucks.*, vol.25 (1983), pp.142-7.
4   D. Ashcroft, *Rec. Bucks.*, vol.13, part 6 (1939), pp.398-426.
5   K. Branigan, *Rec. Bucks.*, vol.18, part 4 (1969), pp.261-76.
6   K. Rutherford Davis, *Britons and Saxons: The Chiltern Region 400-700* (Phillimore, 1982)
7   Appendix 1, BRO, ref. BAS ST 122.
8   A. Baines, *Rec. Bucks.*, vol.23 (1981), pp.76-101.

Chapter Two
1   J. Morris (ed.), *Domesday Book vol.13, Buckinghamshire* (Phillimore, 1978).
2   M. Wood, *Domesday, A Search for the Roots of England* (1986).
3   L. Bull, *Rec. Bucks.*, vol.20, part 1 (1975), pp.87-92.
4   G. Lipscomb, *History and Antiquities of the County of Buckingham*, vol.2 (1847).
5   Public Record Office, *Transcripts of the Register of Edward the Black Prince 1359*, Folio 192.
6   F.H. Pavry and G.M. Knocker, *Rec. Bucks.*, vol.16, part 3 (1957-8), pp.131-78.
7   G. Beresford, 'The Old Manor, Askett', *Rec. Bucks.*, vol.18, part 5 (1971)
8   Bodleian Library, Browne Willis Mss. 1, pp.696-7.
9   N. Pevsner and E. Williamson, *The Buildings of England: Buckinghamshire*, 2nd edition (1994).
10   A. Oswald, 'Country Houses Old and New', *Country Life* (2 September 1933), pp.228-32.
11   Appendix 2, Copyhold admission of 1770.
12   BRO, *Mildmay Papers* ref. M43.
13   *Ibid.*, M43: 15M50/1515.
14   J. van der Graaf, *From the Tithings of Princes Risborough* (1993) private publication.

Chapter Three
1   Bodleian Library, Browne Willis Mss 1, pp.696-7.
2   Chiltern and Chilton both described that part of the parish on the slopes and top of the hills.
3   J. van der Graaf, *From the Tithings of Risborough* (1993).

4   E.J. Evans, *Tithes, Maps, Apportionments and the 1836 Act* (1993).
5   Appendix 3 Letter from the Rev. John Shepherd.
6   B.J. Chubb, *Pauper Migration to the Industrial North from Bledlow* (1996) unpublished thesis.
7   T.W. Davis, *The Enclosure of the Parish of Princes Risborough 1823* (1950) deposited in BRO.
8   Minutes of Princes Risborough Vestry 1830-34.
9   D. Kessler, *The Rothschilds and Disraeli in Buckinghamshire* (1996).
10   BRO Ma/41/2R.

Chapter Four
1   Anon., *A ballad written on the occasion of a Signal Triumph of Thomas Wright* (1877).
2   BRO PR 175/8/10.
3   G. Lipscomb, *Hist. Buck.*, vol.2, p.433.

Chapter Five
1   Buckinghamshire was transferred to the diocese of Oxford in 1854.
2   Bodleian Library, Browne Willis Mss. I, pp.696-7.
3   BRO PR 175/6/1A-B.
4   BRO PR 175/6/3-6A.
5   G. Lipscomb, *The History and Antiquities of the County of Buckingham* (1847).
6   BRO PR 175/6/12.
7   *The People*, 12 May 1907.
8   BRO 15/M50/1394.
9   BRO CCM53.
10   BRO CCM54.
11   J.J. Sheehan, *History and Topography of Buckinghamshire* (1869).
12   *Murray's Buckinghamshire Guide* (1948).

Chapter Six
1   F.H. Pavry, personal communication.
2   BRO Constable's presentments to Quarter Sessions.
3   BRO Quarter Sessions Records.
4   A. Tindal Hart, *The Man in the Pew* (1966), p.142.
5   D. Foster, *The Rural Constabulary Act 1839* (1982).

Chapter Seven
1   W.E. Tate, *The Parish Chest*, 3rd edn (Phillimore, 1983).

2   Bodleian Library, Browne Willis, *op.cit.*
3   BRO PR 175/19/1.
4   BRO PR 175/18/1.

Chapter Eight

1   G. Lipscomb, *History and Antiquities of the County of Buckingham* (1847).
2   J. Lloyd Hart, *Health in the Vale of Aylesbury* (1979).
3   R.A. Kidd, *Transcripts of Princes Risborough Parish Records in BRO.*
4   *Princes Risborough Vestry Minutes, 1830-4.*
5   *Ibid.*
6   *Ibid.*
7   BRO PR 175/18/4.
8   BRO PR 175/18/5.

Chapter Nine

1   E. Thomas, *The Icknield Way*, Wildwood edn. (1980).
2   L. Bull, *A King's Highway* (1978).
3   St J. Priest, *Survey of Bucks* (1813).
4   K. Edmonds, J. Elding and J. Mellor, 'Turnpike Roads of Bucks', *Rec. Bucks.*, vol.35 (1993).
5   J.F. Head, 'An important early valley route through the Chilterns', *Rec. Bucks.*, vol.19 (1974).
6   BRO Spencer Bernard MSS.
7   E17//88 Case relative to Branch of road from Risborough to Thame.
8   BRO D/BNT/104 Alscot map post 1838.

Chapter Ten

1   J.S. Holden, *The Watlington Branch* (1974).
2   R. Lingard, *Princes Risborough-Thame-Oxford Railway* (1978).

Chapter Eleven

1   *Pigot & Co's Directory* (1830).
2   L. Bull, 'Icknield Way Halfway House' private publication.
3   *Evening Standard* and *St James's Gazette* (see Foreword).
4   R.A.D. Bell, personal communication.

Chapter Twelve

1   BRO, British School Log E/LB/175/2; National School Logs 1865-1913 PR 175/25/18-20; Evening Continuation School Log 1898-1928 PR 175/25/28.
2   *Bucks Herald*, 4 January 1862, p.8.

Chapter Thirteen

1   A. Tindal Hart, *The Man in the Pew* (1966), p.27.
2   R. Gibbs, *The Buckinghamshire Miscellany* (1891).
3   W. Keal, 'The Princes Cinema', a tape-recorded conversation with Mr. Len Wright.
4   'The Motor', 29 March 1922, p.321.

Chapter Fourteen

1   BRO, Quarter Sessions, Chepping Wycombe Easter 1698.
2   R. Gibbs, *The Buckinghamshire Miscellany* (1891).
3   *Bucks Free Press*, 9 January 1869.
4   L.W. Kentish, Lt. Col. DSO, *Home Guard Bux 4.*

Epilogue

1   G. Eland, *In Bucks* (1923), p.40.
2   B.J. Rendle, *Fifty Years of Timber Research* (1976).
3   BRO, Princes Risborough National School Log.

Appendix One

1   BRO ST 122.

Appendix Three

1   T.W. Davis, *The Enclosure of Princes Risborough*, thesis deposited at BRO.
2   Prov. 14: 31 He who oppresses the poor insults his Maker; he who is generous to the needy honours Him.
3   Prov. 22: 2.3 Never rob a helpless man because he is helpless, nor ill treat a poor wretch in court; for the Lord will take up their cause and rob him who robs them of their livelihood.
4   8th Commandment Thou shalt not bear false witness against thy neighbour.

Index